THE COMPLETE GUIDE TO
ENDURANCE RIDING AND COMPETITION

THE COMPLETE GUIDE TO
ENDURANCE RIDING AND COMPETITION

DONNA SNYDER-SMITH

Howell Book House

New York

Howell Book House
Hungry Minds
909 Third Avenue
New York, NY 10022

For general information on Hungry Minds' products and services please contact our Customer Care Department within the U.S. at 800-762-2974, outside the U.S. at 317-572-3993 or fax 317-572-4002.

Copyright © 1998 by Donna Snyder-Smith

Library of Congress Cataloging-in-Publication Data

Snyder-Smith, Donna.

The complete guide to endurance riding and competition / Donna Snyder-Smith.

p.   cm.

Includes bibliographical references and index.

ISBN 0-87605-284-7

Endurance riding (Horsemanship) 2. Endurance riding

(Horsemanship)—Competitions.   I. Title

SF296.E5S59   1998

798.2'4—dc21   97-46179

CIP

Manufactured in the United States of America

10 9 8 7 6 5 4

Book Design: George McKeon
Cover Design: Kevin Hanek

This book is dedicated with gratitude to all the horses who have borne my ignorance while they educated me, to my mustangs who so graciously accept the mantle of their captivity to share the secrets of their wild hearts, and to the students who have allowed me to play a role in their pursuit of their dreams.

CONTENTS

FOREWORD

Even though I have won a World Championship and am considered by some to be a leader in the sport of endurance riding, I still look upon myself as a student of both the sport and, more importantly, the horse. For more than two decades I have worked with, conditioned and successfully competed a variety of equine athletes. Each horse, through its individual set of unique challenges, has played a part in my education and ultimate success

A horse named Fire was the catalyst that brought me to Donna Snyder-Smith. Her teaching has guided me to a whole new dimension in equine education, changing my views, my riding, and my training techniques. I have known horsemen as knowledgeable as Donna, but none with her ability to offer information in a way that is so easy to understand, accept and implement. Her ability to communicate is truly a gift.

Now, in this book, Donna shares her experiences and knowledge with everyone. While her perspectives and way of expressing ideas are refreshingly unique, readers who have participated in other equine disciplines will clearly hear the classical principles of horsemanship, like a well-known refrain, within its pages. I trust it will be an enlightening source of information, opening new dimensions of education for each reader.

VALERIE KANAVY
Individual Endurance Gold Medalist
World Equestrian Games 1994

Individual Silver Medalist
World Endurance Championships 1996

INTRODUCTION

It is a race over a marked course against time, gravity, the elements, your own mind and even the forces of aging. This is the sport called endurance riding. One would think it a sport for the young, since riding 25 to 100 miles in a single day is its principle feature, but it is not. Most participants are over thirty. Many are in their fifties and sixties and just getting into the sport. Some compete well past retirement age, like the Grande Dame of Endurance Riding Julie Suhr, and her husband, Bob, whose combined lifetime mileage (37,000 miles), if ridden in a straight line, would have led them more than one and a half times around the world by now.

World-class events like the 100 Mile One Day Tevis Cup Ride and the Old Dominion Ride challenge horse-and-rider teams with extreme topographical and climatic conditions, and rank with famous sporting events such as the Ironman Triathlon and the Iditarod Sled Dog Race in their tests of endurance and spirit. For the novice, local rides offer a great excuse to camp out for a night, ride new trails, and meet interesting people with the same passion.

Endurance riders travel from dawn to dusk in the company of a creature who offers strength without brutality, companionship without criticism, and beauty without vanity. Some view the sport and what it asks of them with fear and wonder. For these participants, *to finish* is to win, no matter where or how often they cross the start and finish lines. For some, the interest in the trail is pragmatic, they must best it to win and winning is the goal. Still others are drawn by history, stories of outlaws fleeing from the hangman's noose, of Indians vanishing like smoke into the wilderness, of cowboy, cavalry scout and mountain man surviving by their wits. The adventure is their prize and arriving at the finish line is an anticlimax.

Since its birth as a sport on this continent in the mid-1950s, endurance riding has continued to thrive and grow, increasing in numbers of both rides and riders, and expanding into other countries with an internationally contested World Championship venue. The sport offers a level playing field between the sexes—testing courage, cunning, stamina, skill and intelligence. Understandably, it attracts the individualist.

THE SPORT OF ENDURANCE RIDING

Most riders start the sport with a horse they already own. Most horses, if they are fit (currently doing a discipline that requires them to be worked two hours a day at least four days a week, with perhaps a three- to four-hour trail ride once a week), conformationally well balanced (or at least not significantly different from good conformational standards), conditioned correctly and ridden within their limits during the event, will be able to complete a 50-mile ride over a moderate course on an average day without undue risk of injury or permanent deterioration. This is true of most performance breeds.

EVALUATING AND SELECTING THE ENDURANCE PROSPECT

The breed that has the best track record in endurance riding is the Arabian. There may be a number of reasons for this, but most certainly one of the strongest is that when you put a horse to work continuously for up to twenty-four hours, you inevitably cause its core temperature to rise. The Arabian's ability to cool itself efficiently (lots of large blood vessels close to the surface, which is covered with very thin skin) comes through its genetic inheritance. The breed was, after all, developed and refined in the desert, and asked to endure extreme heat and hardship throughout all but its most recent history.

1

R.O. Grand Sultan (Rio), 14.3-hand bay Arabian gelding. His record: 9000 + miles, two Tevis wins, two Race of Champions wins and three World Championships. Photo of Rio taken at age 19 winning the Best Condition Award at the 1996 World Championships.

◄

KJ Destination, 15-hand, 13-year-old gray Arabian gelding. He won Best Condition in the Race of Champions two years in a row, finished Top Ten in the North American Championships, and was on the Gold Medal Team at the World Championships in 1996. ➤

Mustang Hawk, 15.2-hand, seven-year-old bay Mustang gelding, 800+ miles. Consistent Top Ten finisher in his second year of 50-mile races.

◄

Mustang Drummer Boy, 15-hand, nine-year-old chestnut Mustang gelding, 650 miles. He has finished 100 percent of his starts. ➤

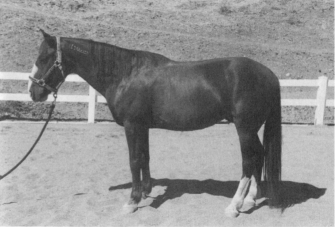

The Thoroughbred, a direct descendant of the Arabian, is also efficient at cooling its body. However, its greater size, generally longer and less dense bone (compared to its Arabian ancestors) and the size and nature of the hoof (which comes as part of the package on most Thoroughbred horses of race-specific breeding), have limited the breed's success in the endurance field.

The Appaloosa, as it was once bred, tough, rangy, with good feet and (often) a stubborn temperament, has proven its merit in endurance but in numbers too small (compared to the Arabian breed) to cause it to be sought out as a breed for the sport. If you are an Appaloosa fan, go for it; just select or evaluate your prospect carefully. If your Appaloosa is a Quarter Horse with spots, its chances of doing well in endurance riding, especially if you hope to compete at speeds beyond the "just to finish" range, are limited.

Quarter Horses, with only a few exceptions, have not found the sport to their liking. Their typically chunky muscling acts as an armor plate through which heat has a great deal of difficulty escaping. Many of today's Quarter Horse lines have a strong infusion of Thoroughbred blood and have inherited the Thoroughbred hoof, which is better suited to groomed tracks or show ring surfaces than to miles and miles of punishing trails over rocks, gravel, sand and mud. Tennessee Walkers and other gaited horses such as Saddlebreds, Paso Finos and Icelandics are not in evidence in great numbers at finish lines. That is not to say that the individual horse of any one of these breeds might not be properly prepared and able to complete rides year after year. Much of that is up to the rider and trainer and to some extent the area of the country in which you intend to compete. Generally speaking, gaited breeds do well on flat to gently rolling trails but do not handle steep climbs and descents easily, especially if an entire ride is comprised of extreme topography. They can not compete with the Arabian on this field of battle

The American Mustang, while not in evidence in great numbers, has managed to establish itself as a contender in endurance riding (a mustang has won the prestigious Tevis Cup and others have been among the top ten in this tough event as well as other rides). Mustangs are noted for their hardy constitution and tough-mindedness, strong bones, good feet and sure-footedness. While they have generally given the best showing against the Arabian at 100-mile distances, Mustang Hawk, a seven-year-old BLM mustang, has finished in the top ten in numerous 50-mile races where the starting fields ranged from 80 to 200 other horses, most of which were Arabians.

Mules also have a strong record in the endurance field, although more as finishers than as front-runners. Morgans are represented in endurance in greater numbers on the East Coast than on the West Coast, and have done particularly well in Canada, where the breeding programs aim at the "sport horse" type rather than the show-ring prima donna.

Conformation

Good conformation is good conformation, and since so many books exist on the subject, I will not give a detailed description of all the aspects sought by horsemen and women the world over. You have only to pick up a copy of *The United States Pony Club Manual of Horsemanship C Level* by Susan Harris or *The Equine Athlete* by Jo Hodges and Sarah Pilliner and study what is written there to become strong enough in the basics of conformation and movement analysis to avoid glaring mistakes in the selection of a horse for the sport of endurance. You can also save yourself from wasting a great amount of time preparing a currently owned mount for the endurance-riding discipline that would better be left in the show ring or on the pleasure trail. What I would like to add to the general body of knowledge specifically about endurance horses is the following:

- They come in all different shapes and sizes, but the best average between 14.2 and 15.2 hands.
- Good ones have a deep heart girth with lots of lung capacity, a clean throatlatch, a large windpipe and big nostrils.
- *They like what they do.*
- They have well-shaped, tough feet that are the same size and symmetry, and are open at the heels.
- They are balanced or "uphill" in their skeletal structure and in their movement.
- *They like what they do.*
- Their chest is neither wide nor narrow.
- They have powerful hindquarters, sloping shoulders and short-to medium-length pasterns.
- Neither their elbows nor their stifles "hug" their bodies.
- *They like what they do.*

Attitude

Attitude may seem less important than bone structure and coupling, and perhaps it is from a certain perspective. But I guarantee you that when you are on top of an overly emotional animal that is leaping about at the starting line, your mount's bone structure will not be foremost in your mind. Neither will attitude seem a minor point when your horse jigs sideways down the trail for several miles during a controlled start, or when stuck behind a slower horse on a single-track trail. Having your arms pulled out of their sockets by a horse lungeing against the reins for 20 miles as you fight to keep it from running itself into a state of collapse isn't much fun either. A stable mind is just as important as a strong body. Indeed, without a stable mind, the body, despite the best of training and care, will inevitably sustain much greater strain during competition if not during the entire conditioning process. For this reason, attitude and temperament must be considered high on the list of desirable traits in the prospective endurance horse and should be focused on during its training.

In considering attitude, I would refuse a horse that cribbed, stall (or paddock) walked, windsucked, pawed excessively when tied, or pulled back when tied. While some of these behaviors can be cleared up or reduced with time, training and sometimes a change in routine (for instance, turning a stalled horse out to pasture), they are clear signs that the horse is less than stable mentally. The training road to success in endurance is several years long when done right, and emotional problems will only serve to lengthen it or lead to disaster. A case in point is the stall walker who, after being purchased, is turned out. If this horse and rider were selected for a National or International Championship, the horse would have to be confined to a stall for at minimum of three to five days. It would be considerably longer if the championship was off-continent and the horse had to be quarantined before being shipped. When the horse finds himself confined again, the old behavior patterns most likely will return and the horse may stall walk or weave for the entire time. Such behavior threatens not only the rider's chances of success, but those of the team as well. The stress this horse will put himself through could easily cause him to become lame either before or during the event. A horse that kicks when it is confined, either in a stall or trailer, presents a similar problem.

No one plans to spend the time and money training and hauling a horse, surviving the normal pitfalls of the sport, to have their horse self-destruct. But kidding yourself by down-playing the potential impact of undesirable behavior (bad habits) is a good way to find yourself in this very situation.

Night Vision

If you plan to ride 100-mile rides the horse's night vision should be checked, and—if your choice is an Appaloosa—perhaps even "test driven." Being able to rely on your horse's night vision is a matter of safety as well as a matter of finding the next vet check/finish line.

Legs and Movement

Everyone talks about straight legs. I certainly would recommend getting the straightest-legged horse that the market and your pocketbook allow you to acquire. However, after over thirty years of selecting, training and competing a wide variety of horse breeds in a number of athletically demanding disciplines such as jumping, eventing, and endurance riding, what I have observed is this: Many champions in all those disciplines have less than straight legs, while some have marked deviations in straightness and yet do an excellent job in their sport, remaining sound year after year. What I have sometimes also observed is that one deviation in the leg/bone structure is offset somewhere above or below in the continuing leg column or the connective joints, and the two "faults" seem to cancel each other out in action. Occasionally they do more than simply cancel each other out: they make the horse an anomaly, a superior mover or performer despite outward appearances. What is important in any horse whose legs must take sustained concussion is (1) that cannon bones are more short than long and the bone is dense and flat; (2) that knees are flat and in line with the rest of the leg structure, giving the appearance when viewed from the side, of a straight, somewhat tapering line down both the front of the leg and the back of the leg to the fetlock joint (the knee when viewed in this manner should not "pop" forward or appear to sink back); (3) that the tendon that attaches to the back of the knee should not be tied in, making the line at the back of the leg appear to have a jog in it just behind and below the knee joint; and (4) the legs should be attached "one on each corner" of the horse, giving it the appearance of a well-balanced table.

It is just as important to study the flight and landing pattern of the foot when the horse is in motion at the different gaits as it is to study the bony alignments when it is standing still, and indeed, perhaps even more revealing of the horse's suitability to the job. A good endurance horse is an efficient mover. The horse that spends a lot of energy lifting its knees in the air at any gait, but particularly at trot and canter, is wasting energy that could better be used in covering ground. Thoroughbred folks call an efficient mover a *daisy cutter*, meaning the horse swings its feet rather than lifting them. A horse's way of going (movement patterns) can, to some degree, be changed by training and shoeing, but movement dictated by skeletal structure can not be radically changed without sooner or later damaging the horse's structure.

A horse that stands base narrow (the width between the feet is less than the width of the shoulders) often wings. This action (foot-flight pattern) can cause it to strike one foot or leg with another, injuring itself. Such patterns usually increase (worsen) as the horse tires. A horse that stands basewide or is pigeon-toed will tend to paddle (swing the leg outward), moving the foot from the shoulder. While less likely to damage its own legs, a horse with this pattern of movement is less desirable as an endurance horse because it wastes energy when it moves.

An interesting note on mustang movement: All the ones I have encountered have a gait I call the *mustang shuffle*. It is a very slow jog that seems to require almost no energy and that they can keep up all day long. I strongly suspect it is their natural gait for getting from place to place in the wild, and since it has almost no bounce even though it is a true diagonal trot, it is also very comfortable for the rider.

Body Balance

When evaluating a horse for endurance, whether it be your own or a prospective purchase, evaluate the body for symmetry. Asymmetrical development or gait is often a sign of pain, either current or long standing. A horse that is uncomfortable somewhere in its body, but is worked because it is not overtly lame, will protect itself the only way it can—by using the painful part of its body less and other compensating parts more. So bear in mind that overdevelopment patterns you observe may be the result of a problem far removed from the source of the pain. Example, a horse that is sore in both front feet may appear to move evenly when trotted for soundness, but when observed standing, you can see an other-than-normal body posture in its stance. The horse may place its hind legs further underneath itself to help take the pressure off its sore front feet. If this is a long-standing condition, the muscles of its hindquarters may be overly developed *when compared to its forequarters.*

Look over your prospect carefully, comparing one side of the horse to the other. Overdevelopment or atrophication are clues to current soundness as well as to the likelihood of the horse staying sound.

Whether you define success as the ability to accumulate a lifetime mileage record into the tens of thousands of miles, the ability to cross the finish line first or the winning of a gold medal, the endurance horse needs

- Good feet

- A good respiratory system

- A good mind

- To be an efficient mover

- The desire to do it

Matching Horse and Rider

The rider's conformation should be considered in selecting an endurance prospect. Finding a good physical horse/rider match will affect things like safety, comfort, balance, control and long-term soundness. When balanced and skillful, the well-proportioned middleweight rider can comfortably ride the greatest variety of horses.

A small rider with short legs will have trouble feeling comfortable on a wide horse.

If you are a short rider, in the 4 foot-11 inch to 5 foot-2 inch range, you probably have short legs and arms and would be more comfortable on a small, slender horse with a medium to short neck. Having to climb a 16-hand mountain every time you mount on the trail can be tiring and a big-strided horse's momentum/suspension will be hard for a small rider to stay balanced over, especially at the posting trot. If you are short-legged, straddling a wide-barreled horse for 100 miles can cause strain in your hip joints and can stress your lower back. Short legs make it hard to get around a horse's ribs to engage the horse, so a short rider should have a horse built uphill. Such a horse will have less tendency to become forehand-heavy when it tires. Long-legged riders won't be comfortable on a narrow horse. They will feel as though they must wrap their legs around the horse's barrel, since their legs won't be able to find a comfortable contact point on the horse's sides otherwise. Tall riders with long legs need a wide horse with a deep barrel. A short-necked horse can easily unbalance a tall rider if it should stop suddenly, lower its neck, buck, or drop a shoulder and turn quickly.

A tall, long-legged rider on a small, short-necked horse will find it hard to maintain balance and feel secure. ➤

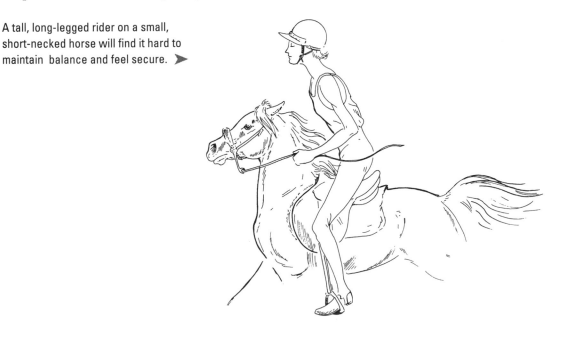

If you are a featherweight and are riding a big, strong, muscular horse, you can expect your body to be a little less persuasive than if you had the physical impact of the heavyweight rider. Flies can get a horse's attention by irritating them, but they are not known for their ability to stop a horse dead in its tracks. Rhinos, on the other hand, can do a better job of being an immovable wall in the case of a runaway. If you are a heavyweight rider, it is important to look for a short-coupled horse with a broad, well-muscled loin, since that is the type of horse most capable of carrying weight for long distances/periods of time without developing back problems.

The heavyweight's horse should be short-coupled with a wide, strong loin, or it may develop back problems. ➤

Considering Your Goals

When buying a horse for endurance, your timetable for participating in the sport, as well as the level (ride distances) to which you aspire will affect your search. If you want to ease yourself into the sport, starting with 25-mile rides (Limited Distance Division) and perhaps have the pleasure of developing your equine partner yourself, you will shop for a young horse between three and a half and five years of age. Your priorities are good movement, good body balance, good bone, straight legs, great feet, a stable mind and a personality you want to spend time with. The horse will have little or no experience and you will start the training and conditioning process from scratch. You can expect one to two years of long, slow, distance work, depending on the age of the horse, then a season of competitive trail or limited-distance competition. You may want to split your horse's first 50-mile season with a few early limited-distance rides and then move up to 50s. You can move up to a 70- to 100-mile ride at the end of the ride season in the horse's second competitive year if the horse is getting stronger and your goal is to do 100-mile events. This would put your horse in the fall of his sixth (birth) year before his first 100-mile ride. If you want to stay at the 50-mile distance and go faster (and your horse is capable of it), you would begin to ride your horse to the front in its third year of competition. If you are looking to jump right into competition in either 50- or 100-milers, you will be looking for a mature horse, from seven to twelve years old, with a history of two solid years of successful ride completions. It needs to be sound and conformationally constructed to stay that way, sane (as that will affect your enjoyment of the sport as well as insure or diminish the chances of the horse staying sound into the future) with a substantiated paper trail, showing

- How often it was competed in the past.

- How often it completed or was pulled (times should improve from the beginning of the season to the end of the season, or at least from one season to the next).

- What the time period was between rides (long periods without competition could signal a serious injury that required the horse to be rested).

- What the ride distances were.

- What the riding times were for each ride/race.

- Where the horse finished (first, top ten, best condition, etc.).

- What distances the horse was hauled to rides.

- How it did in rides where it was hauled long distances as compared to how it placed in closer events (this will give you a pretty accurate reading on whether the horse is a good traveler).

- What the topography and altitude were at its events, especially in events where it did exceptionally well.

- What types of weather and footing conditions it has competed in (humidity? sand? rocks?).

- How many different riders the horse has competed with.

- What weight of rider it has carried during competition.

- What weight of rider it is used to carrying when in training.

Knowing how to read a paper trail allows you to select the horse that can successfully take you to the level of competition you wish to try. A word of caution: The sport of endurance riding is a *partnership*. You can't skip to the top by buying a top-flight horse. You must also become an experienced top-flight partner if you want to participate at the toughest, most challenging level.

You can expect a horse with lots of experience, success and soundness to cost more than a young, unconditioned prospect. While it is possible to find an acceptable, registered Arabian gelding in some parts of the country for as little as fifteen hundred dollars, don't be surprised if the proven performer brings between six and ten thousand dollars. Winning, international-caliber endurance horses have already been sold for six-figure prices. The great thing about endurance is, if you can't afford a horse with a big price tag, you can buy a good young one; do your homework and with some time and a little luck you may end up with a horse that someone else thinks is worth a million dollars and that you won't consider parting with for any amount of money!

The Veterinary Exam

Whether you are buying a horse for endurance or thinking about having your horse make a career change, it would be a wise idea to have the horse thoroughly checked by an experienced endurance vet. If possible, choose one who not only vets lots of rides but also has participated in the sport as a rider. During this exam the normal things such as soundness, heart, lungs and eyes will be checked, but it should also include a fairly vigorous mounted workout for the horse, after which the vet will again check heart and lungs and recovery capacity. A horse's recovery capacity will improve with training, but finding a horse that recovers extremely well before it has had years of conditioning certainly means it will start its career with an advantage. Prepurchase x-rays are a more common practice in sports horse disciplines, such as dressage, jumping and eventing, than in an endurance horse vet check. But even though clean x-rays are not a guarantee of soundness and push the cost of a vet check up by a hundred dollars or more, a good set of x-rays of both the hoof and the lower joints can provide a valuable baseline record if trouble or lameness should occur during the horse's career. When considering the long-term picture and the amount of money you will spend over the next several years training and competing, an investment of one to two hundred dollars can end up saving you several thousands of dollars by keeping you from purchasing a horse that shows early arthritic changes in its feet or joints.

DRESSING FOR ENDURANCE

Endurance, being one of the youngest sports in the equestrian venue, is still quite casual in its approach to a uniform, and indeed has no mandatory dress code such as is found in the dressage, hunter/jumper, eventing or western reining or riding fields.

What riders use is what works for them. This ranges from shorts and tennis shoes to formal riding breeches and boots. A frequent combination is riding tights and over-the-calf socks with a sport-specific riding boot such as the Ariat paddock boot or riding sneakers.

Endurance riders often get off and walk or run with their horses during a ride. Tall riding boots are not a good choice if the rider chooses (or is forced) to do much footwork during a ride. A good riding boot or shoe should offer support and comfort, both in and out of the stirrup. Running shoes are worn by many endurance riders, but they do not have a heel, so rank lower in safety than their cousin, the riding sneaker, which does have a heel. If you use a running shoe, you should also use a stirrup guard. This will prevent your foot from slipping through and becoming locked in the stirrup should you have an accident or a fall.

Endurance riders' feet get wet almost all of the time. You'll dismount in a creek

An endurance rider wearing shorts and running shoes.

to sponge your horse or use a scoop at a water trough, and by the time you're done soaking your horse, your feet will be soaked as well. That being the case, a fabric shoe or boot that offers adequate support, such as the Ariat Freestyle, made of a washable synthetic, is a much better choice than a leather boot.

> An endurance rider's footwear should: (1) fit like a glove; (2) feel extremely comfortable; (3) give the foot support in and out of the stirrup; and (4) offer safety and a good value.

For riders who feel naked without the leg protection of a tall boot, half-chaps or leggings are the answer. Made from regular leather or suede, this calf-length legwear slips on over a shoe or paddock boot, usually with a strap which goes under the arch of the foot, and is fitted to the rider's leg by a zipper or Velcro. Better models have a wide band of elastic at the top and buckle adjustments to help keep them in place.

Since dress is the rider's option, you will see a wide range of clothing, including jeans, shorts, breeches, riding tights and schooling sweats. Riding tights are recommended because they are designed to be both comfortable (they stretch, insuring a snug but comfortable fit) and practical (no unnecessary seams).

Riding tights come in a variety of fabrics, including cotton/Lycra and nylon/Lycra as well as Polarfleece for cold-weather riding and often come with pads both at the knee and in other strategic places for comfort. Two popular brands of riding tights are Carousel Action Wear and Saddle Bums.

A rider at the Michigan Bluff vet check wearing the most popular endurance outfit: riding tights, running shoes, long-sleeved lightweight shirt, and a safety helmet with a protective sun drape.

◄

Loose pants tend to shift position, ride up, and wrinkle, and can cause chafing and irritation. If you find your pants are causing you a problem during a ride, try wearing a pair of women's pantyhose underneath them. It will help eliminate the chafing problem.

Choosing the right undergarment will be important to your comfort. The best way to find a variety of well-made briefs, jocks, and bras that offer comfort and adequate support is to shop from catalogs, for example, Road Runner Sports. Retail stores that carry biking, hiking, running, skiing and mountain-climbing gear and clothing are also good places to shop for practical, lightweight clothing that will cross over to endurance riding.

Upper-body dress will vary according to weather. While many riders use a fitted, stretch tank top if the weather is hot, a lightweight, long-sleeve shirt worn over it will help protect your skin from sun and dirt. A shirt also offers some protection from brush, biting insects and ticks. Whatever you choose should fit and wear well, feel comfortable, dry quickly, breathe, and be easy to clean. Dressing in layers is always a smart move since even in warm climates, rides that begin before dawn and end after dark could have a wide range of temperature changes, requiring a jacket, windbreaker or even some form of rain gear. Wool in cold climates can be itchy, but it has the ability to hold warmth if wet. When warmth is desired, Polarfleece is a much better choice than down. Keep in mind if you do use a synthetic fiber, you want it to breathe like natural fiber does.

Riding with a helmet is advisable and with today's new lightweight, well-ventilated helmets (unlike old helmets that were very hot and heavy), there is no excuse not to avail yourself of this safety advantage. Helmets not only protect the head in case of an accident but also offer the scalp protection from sunburn. Breakaway visors help shade your eyes. If the weather is hot you can wet a small thin sponge (the type found in any grocery store) and place it under your helmet to stay cool. In winter, helmets help keep you warm by holding in heat, especially if you add a wool headband that covers your ears underneath your helmet. Many rides encourage the wearing of a helmet, but there is no rule that makes wearing one mandatory.

Socks are a part of the "happy feet" picture. My recommendation is the over-the-calf kind usually found in the menswear departments of better department stores. Cotton socks are absorbent, but thick ones can get bunched up inside boots and become uncomfortable. Wool socks are warm, but work best if a light cotton sock is worn underneath to absorb perspiration, because your feet will sweat even in cold weather. Nylon socks are thin, fit the best, but offer no protection against rubs and have no moisture-absorbing capacity. Specialty socks designed for other outdoor sports that utilize various fibers to wick, dry, pad, or warm your foot and leg can be found at sports-specific stores.

With today's everwidening and sensitive sports clothing market many riders enjoy putting together distinctive, colorful outfits to suit their personality or their mood. If you are used to the formal dress and colors of show ring sports, the haute couture of endurance may surprise or even shock you (leopard riding tights and tank top) but the bright colors of endurance, like a quick-moving hummingbird, have their place in equestrian fashion.

The American Endurance Ride Conference (AERC)

AERC is the governing and sanctioning body for endurance riding in this country. The stated purpose of this organization is to promote the sport of endurance riding, to act as an education center and clearing house for information concerning endurance riding, and to encourage better care of endurance horses and the prevention of cruelty to animals. (The organization is headquartered at 11960 Heritage Oak Place, Suite 9, Auburn, CA 95603; phone 530-823-2260) Its rules dictate the conduct of riders, vets, and ride management at endurance events in the United States. Riders wishing to enter a sanctioned endurance event at distances of 50 miles or greater must be members of AERC or pay a ten-dollar nonmember fee, plus their ride entry. Riders who are not members of AERC can currently enter the Limited Distance Division (25 to 35 miles) of an AERC event (if the shorter division is offered) without a penalty, but becoming a member of AERC has a lot of advantages.

AERC keeps track of the lifetime mileage of its members. (When you join you will receive a member number which will follow you through your years of competition and which is required as a part of the information that is called for on your entry form for all sanctioned rides). You can also register your horse in AERC's lifetime mileage program. When you do this, your horse will receive his own number. Regional and National Awards are given each year at the Annual Convention and Trade Show (usually held in Reno, Nevada, in late January or early February). Awards include a Rider Mileage Program,

1000 Mile Horse Program, Limited Distance Rider Mileage and Limited Distance Horse Mileage Program, Top Ten Regional Weight Division Awards, Regional Junior Division and National top twenty placing in National mileage, Best Condition, National 100 Mile Award, Jim Jones (stallions) Award, Bill Thornburgh Family Award (family with most miles during ride season), Husband/Wife Team Award, and the Bill Stuckey Award (riders sixty-five years and over with the greatest mileage).

- AERC recognizes four weight divisions. All weight divisions include the weight of the rider and their tack:

    Featherweight—under 160 pounds

    Lightweight—161 to 185 pounds

    Middleweight—186 to 210 pounds

    Heavyweight—over 210 pounds

- Horses must be at least four years old to enter the Limited Distance Division on an AERC-sanctioned ride, and at least five years of age to enter rides of 50 miles or more.

- All horses must be shod.

- Rides are open to any breed.

- Any horses that show evidence of the administration of abnormal substances or normal substances in abnormal amounts are prohibited from competition.

The sport offers a variety of competitive levels. They are

- Local rides in the Limited Distance Division: 25 to 30 miles in six hours, usually held in conjunction with a 50-mile ride.

- Local 50-mile rides: Twelve-hour completion time.

- Local 100-mile rides: 24 hours to complete, local events usually have a relaxed atmosphere.

- Special Event 100-mile rides with qualifying requirements such as the Race Of Champions: Party atmosphere, lots of excitement and tough competition. Many riders enter this ride for the honor of competing against the best in the sport.

- Special Event 100-mile rides with an open entry such as the Tevis and Old Dominion: Usually attract entries because of the toughness of the trail and their place in the history of the sport.

- AERC Championship Series Rides: 100 miles in 24 hours, against other top competitors for the yearly National Championship titles in the various recognized weight divisions.

- Multi-Day Rides: Usually 50 miles a day for two to five days in a row, generally held in scenic, historic wilderness areas.

- International Events: 100-mile events that require nomination procedures, selection by a committee, horse passports, and so forth. The North American Championships, the European Championships and the World Endurance Championships are events at this level. It looks like the same critter, but it isn't. The top horses and riders in the world compete here. Strategy and political red tape are a part of the game as are incredible excitement and pressure. It is a great high just to be selected, but it means lots of work and requires a much greater investment of time and money than riding at the local level. The ultimate reward here is finishing sound with a Gold Medal or two as a representative of your country and sport.

The AERC yearly convention is an event that features informative lectures about the sport with up-to-date information on the care and training of the long-distance equine athlete, as well as a venue for presenting year-end awards. This is an excellent place for the novice or entry-level endurance rider or "wannabe" to learn about the sport and to meet the people already involved. It also offers a trade show that is not to be topped for its array of the latest and best for both horse and rider. With many saddle makers on hand, the show provides easy access to a variety of saddles designed specifically for the trail rider and allows you to compare different kinds of saddles before you choose the one that best suits your needs and the needs of your horse.

Endurance News is the monthly magazine that is mailed to members of AERC. It includes informative articles about the personalities and issues of the sport and a comprehensive ride calendar by region (there are eight U.S. regions) listing ride date, location (state and region), name, distance(s), and the organizer's (contact person's) name, address and telephone number. It also keeps track of yearly point standings for riders who are competing for the year-end awards, and ride results for every sanctioned ride held in the United States.

The ride result section is particularly useful for assessing the difficulty of unfamiliar rides around your local area and the rest of the country as well. Information in this section includes the number of starting and finishing riders (on difficult rides the finishing number of riders will range between 50 and 70 percent of those starting), the fastest finishing time (the winner's riding time) and the time it took the final rider to complete the ride. If the winner took only three and one half hours to complete a 50-mile race, and the final rider completed in eight hours, it is a good bet that the ride can be qualified as an "easy" ride. On the other hand, if the first-place finisher on a 50 took six and a half hours and the last place finisher just made the cutoff time of twelve hours, the ride is tough because of terrain, footing or weather, or all three. Ride results identifies the ride by name, place and date, and gives the winner and the winner of the Best Condition Award by name, the listing by place, and—for all ride participants—the rider's name, horse's name, and completion time and points. Statistics fans will find this information useful in exploring the records of top endurance riders and their horses. Watching the progression (in elapsed racing times at the same event) from year to year and noting which rides they choose to progress their horses is a way of gathering valuable "insider" training information.

AERC also publishes an annual yearbook and gives interval awards such as mileage patches (250-mile to 1000-mile intervals, then every 1000 miles thereafter) to its members, as well as 1000-mile medallions to member's horses. New members also receive the *Endurance Riders Handbook*, (an excellent how-to book edited by winning endurance competitor Nina Warren) and a copy of the rules.

The AERC is governed by a board of directors, elected by the membership. The board deals with questions of rules, ethics, safety and the overall promotion of the sport. The organization has procedures for protest, just like the American Horse Shows Association, and rules against the use of drugs. The office staff is user-friendly and is happy to answer questions from riders new to the sport, as well as from long-time members.

Be a Good Partner— Be a Balanced Rider

Riders need to find and maintain their balance without using a lot of muscle tension if they want their horse to do its best. To use "body speak" (hands, legs, seat and weight) to control the horse, riders must be able to use different parts of their body independently. Your body speak to the horse needs to be clear if you expect the horse to understand and cooperate. When your body speak says, "I'd like you to slow down a bit," and your horse answers, "Forget it, I'm going to pass that flea-bitten gray thug in front of us whose mother was the daughter of a camel," it is your ability to use your hands, seat and legs in a coordinated and independent manner that will allow you to regain *control*, win the battle of opinions, and keep yourself aboard. In order to do this, you must be able to keep yourself in balance as the horse is trying to hurtle you forward at cannonball speed. Body speak can be polite (half-halts) or if necessary, more emphatic ("Slow down before I tear all your teeth out").

Whether polite or strong, to be effective, the rider must enunciate the aids clearly without stuttering. Clear, effective body speak is not possible when the rider is locked up with tension. Imagine you are sitting on top of a cliff on a warm day, enjoying the breeze. Now imagine you're dangling over the edge, hands clenched tightly around a rock to keep from plunging to your death.

Do you still think you'd notice the breeze? Feedback from your horse (the breeze) is a necessary part of good/effective communication (use of the aids).

> *Perfect practice makes perfect. If you use the wrong muscles during practice, your body learns the wrong response patterns. That is why it is possible to ride for thousands of hours and/or miles and not become an accomplished rider.*

Being centered or balanced on the horse is different from just hanging on. While hanging on is useful, especially if the alternative is to fall off, hanging on doesn't allow the rider much opportunity to feel. Riding that is comfortable and productive for both horse and rider is based on the rider's ability to feel the horse and what it is doing with its body. I agree staying on top must be the first step, but to be successful as an endurance rider, sooner or later you must move beyond survival and begin to ride from a place of balance and control.

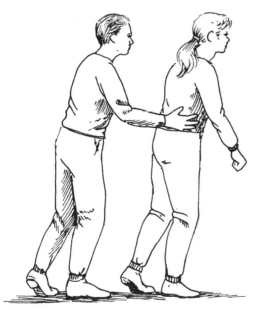

You can ride a horse by grip or you can ride a horse by balance. Both methods work if your only goal is to stay on top. Smart riders will seek to understand the dynamics of each method and choose the one that allows them to make the greatest contribution to their equine partner.

Learning Exercise 1   Grab a friend around the rib cage with the palms of your hands. Let your hands on your partner's rib cage represent your legs around the horse, as they would be when you ride. Now ask your human "horse" to walk, turn and stop while you follow it, keeping the palms of your hands steadily but lightly pressed against each side of its rib cage. To get a good feel for the situation, don't talk about where you want your "horse" to go or when you want it to move, but experiment with pressure from your hands to start, stop and turn it. Ask your friend to notice what he or she is feeling (and thinking) while you do this exercise together and share it with you when your "ride" is done. Now do the experiment again, only this time "grip" your friend's rib cage by pressing the palms of your hands hard against it the whole time you move through the exercise (pretend you are riding a young, green horse, who has spent the last week locked in a stall and that it is a windy day).

Explore the exercise by doing it twice: once as the "rider" and once as the "horse." Compare the two experiences. Which allowed the most ease of movement? Which the best communication? Which produced the most confusion/resistance as reported by the horse? Which was more tiring for horse and rider? The exercise will clearly demonstrate to you, from the rider's point of view as well as the horse's, the advantages of riding in balance rather than riding by grip. Learning this simple fact through bodily experience is the door to becoming a better, more effective rider. Another important piece to this puzzle is the fact that if you grip your horse, you make it difficult, if not impossible, for your horse to lift its back and move in a light, balanced manner.

Learning Exercise 2   To better understand your and your horse's biomechanical function and the impact tension has on it, just drop down on a rug on all fours and pretend to be a horse. Notice how you distribute your weight between your four "legs." Now arch your back, dropping your belly downward towards the floor and take a few steps forward. You can pretend someone just put a saddle on you that gouges you behind the shoulder and presses uncomfortably on the muscles next to your spine, and then she pulled the cinch extra tight. How did it feel when you tried to move with your body in that posture? Stop after a few steps and "round" your back slightly. Notice that you are using your abdominal muscles in raising your back upward toward the ceiling. Now walk forward in this posture. Is it easier or harder than moving with your back hollowed? Why do you suppose the horse would want to go with a hollow back when it is so much easier to move when the back is raised? Try having someone "ride" you when you are in your horse position. If your rider sits lightly and quietly, it isn't too difficult to keep your back raised, and carry them. But if she leans backward, pinches your back, or allows her shoulders to sway from side to side, what happens? How do her actions affect your ability to put your feet where you want to?

- *The good rider sits lightly in the saddle with her feet directly under her at all gaits, as well as at the halt.*

- *The dynamics of position and the correct use of the rider's body interacting with the horse's motion is more important than static form, but without form there is no control.*

- *The most efficient horse is the balanced horse.*

- *It takes more energy to recover balance than to maintain it.*

- *To minimize effort and impact, it is of the utmost importance that the rider be able to move in harmony and noninterference with the horse as it negotiates the wide variety of terrain found in the sport of endurance riding.*

- *True noninterference can only be accomplished by the balanced rider.*

A rider who is not in balance both longitudinally and laterally uses muscle for security. This muscle tension in the rider's body causes a corresponding tension in the horse's body. Consider trotting your horse for a mile on packed sand by the ocean's edge. How much energy did it take to go the distance? How much more energy would it take to go that distance if you and the horse were knee-deep in the ocean while you trotted? Tension, like water, creates resistance to motion. It tires and debilitates and is to be avoided in the trail rider and trail horse whenever possible. Tension is produced when either horse or rider are out of balance. By doing the following exercise, you will teach yourself this lesson so your body as well as your mind can understand the importance of this basic truth. If you read and think about this exercise, your mind will learn; however, if you actually *do* it, your body will learn there is a better way.

Learning Exercise 3   Partly fill your horse's bucket with water. Carry it with you as you take a walk. Notice how much the muscles on the side of your body opposite the hand carrying the bucket are tensing in order to help you maintain your balance. Carry the bucket in front of you. What happens to the muscles of your back when you do this? Move the bucket an arm's length away from you, either to the side or to the front. What does that produce in terms of tension in your body? Now try carrying a bucket in each hand. Keep the buckets close to your body. How does this change the picture?

Balance makes a difference in the amount of effort required to do a job. This is just as true for your horse as it is for you. Horses, despite being so large, are unstable because their center of gravity is high off the ground and because they are much longer than they are wide. It is easy for a rider to unbalance a horse, causing it to work harder. The effect of your interference with your horse's ability to balance itself does not stop with increased effort on the part of your horse during training or competition, but extends to your horse's soundness as well. A horse can feel when it steps in a hole or on a sharp rock. If it is unhindered, it will immediately rebalance itself to prevent the endangered limb from taking weight and becoming injured. But if you are tense, your horse is not free. Instead, your body unwittingly acts as a restraint to your horse's natural movement and your horse is locked into an interactive dance of tension and counterbalance with you, its partner.

BASIC POSITION

To obtain the desired lightness, imagine all your bones above your pelvis are filled with helium. The helium skeleton is constantly "lifting" you, never allowing you to slouch or become heavy. Imagine the parts of your body that touch the saddle are filled with extremely fine sand, like that used in egg timers. The weight of the sand stabilizes you, molding your seat and legs to the saddle and your horse's sides without tension or effort—but because the sand is so fine, it is very mobile, shifting and changing smoothly and evenly as your horse's body moves under you. Let any unnecessary tension drain from your muscles, especially from your neck, shoulders, chest and lower back. This is the beginning of light riding. A heavyweight who sits lightly and in balance stresses a horse less over the miles than a lightweight who is stiff and unbalanced.

When assessing a rider's longitudinal balance, ask yourself this question: If the horse disappeared, would this rider end up standing solidly over her feet on the ground?

On flat or slightly undulating ground, the body of the trail rider is balanced over his or her feet in such a way that a vertical line dropped from the rider's ear passes through the rider's shoulder, hip and ankle at walk, sitting trot or jog, and canter or lope. This line changes when the rider stands or two-points for faster gaits such as the gallop, or for uphill and fast downhill work. At rising trot, gallop, or when doing hill work, the rider's torso inclines forward from the hip joint. To keep the torso balanced over the feet when bringing your shoulders forward, you must allow your hips to slide back in the saddle. This way your shoulders and hips counterbalance each other and your body mass remains over your feet.

Remember, (1) don't push on the stirrups; (2) fold your torso at the hip; and (3) keep your back flat. In the two-point or half-seat position, weight is shifted off your buttocks and redistributed on your inner thighs. The stirrup will receive some of your redistributed weight, but must not bear the entire burden. Never contract the inner thigh muscles, "pinching" the horse. This position can only be accomplished without effort if your stirrup length is short enough to permit you to flex your ankles, knees and hip joints. These flexed joints become your shock absorbers.

A word or two about your kinesthetic sense and the role it plays in learning: Your *kinesthetic sense* is your awareness of your body in space. Unfortunately,

Position 1. The most comfortable body position and stirrup length for walk, jog, and canter or lope. Position 2. The most efficient position and stirrup length for rising trot and moderate incline work. Position 3. The most functional position and stirrup length for gallop and steep hill work. ➤

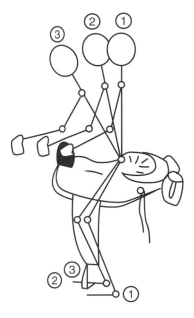

A winning strategy for endurance riding is to change the length of your stirrups during a ride. This changes the amount of work being done by your various muscle groups, resting some while putting others to work. Shorten your stirrups two to three inches before you do prolonged galloping or downhill work. This increases the shock-absorbing capacity of your knees and ankles. Better shock absorbers make the ride easier on you and your horse. Lengthen your stirrups again to rest your leg muscles after the job is done.

the kinesthetic sense can and does become distorted. Consider the seemingly simple task of standing up straight. Most of the students I work with think they know how to stand up straight when they come to me. I put them in front of a full-length mirror and tell them to show me what "straight" looks like. Most people lock their knees and use a lot of muscle tension in the lower back, chest and other parts of their body to hold their torso *behind* their feet. Some even evidence a marked arch in the lower back as a result of this posture. When they think they are standing straight, I ask them to feel the weight distribution in their feet and compare it to the length of the foot from heel to toe. Most reply they feel more of the weight on their heels.

I let them look over their shoulder into the mirror and show them with a plumb line that they are not straight at all. Instead, they are unbalanced with their shoulders to the rear, which is why they feel more of their weight is on their heels. The main reason we don't listen to the obvious (like the feel of where our weight is on our feet) is that our brains have recorded and named the patterns we most frequently use to work, move and stand. In this case, the word that triggers the series of incorrect muscular patterns is "straight." When we are told to stand up straight, we get stuck in all the brain's accumulated pattern input—what your mother or drill instructor told you about "straight," for instance—and fail to notice whether what we are doing has anything to do with actual straightness as it applies to balance and gravity. Getting rid of this false picture often requires help from some outside source, such as the mirror my students used to see that they were actually leaning back when their brain was telling them they were straight.

We are also subject to these incorrect brain "patterns" when we ride. If you are a longtime rider you will have developed very specific patterns in your body about how to do it. This is why it is harder to *break* a pattern than to acquire a new one. As riders, our distorted kinesthetic sense might tell us we are sitting in the middle of our saddle (horse) when actually we are off center to the left or right (a common problem), or it may convince us we are sitting on the vertical when our bodies are actually behind of or in front of that balanced place. If you are used to sitting behind the vertical when you ride and someone tells you to move your torso more forward, you may move a tiny bit to be cooperative, but your brain will prevent you from moving as much as you need to. As you begin to use different muscles to correct your seat and balance, the brain rebels, screaming at you to stop! If you ignore it and continue with your corrections to your position, your brain will try to make you believe you are laying on your horse's neck (too far forward) or leaning way back (too far to the rear) when in fact you are centered over your feet correctly. This happens quite frequently and it is one of the reasons even dedicated riders who read and study have a difficult time improving their own riding/balance skills without the intervention of an instructor or coach. Unless you see photos or a video of yourself while riding, you will doubt what anyone tells you because your brain will try to tell you differently. If you find yourself suffering from a distorted kinesthetic sense, visual input will help you begin to build the trust necessary to make the physical shifts in your body that need to be made. You will need to ignore the feedback from your brain for about a month to change your old habits. Once on your horse, your most reliable source of input about *true* balance (or the lack of it) is the presence or absence of tension in your body, particularly in the areas of your back, chest, shoulders, neck, inner thigh muscles, ankles and feet. If your body is truly balanced, you won't need tension to maintain your position. Good riders appear to flow with their horses because they are in balance and there is no unnecessary tension in their bodies. When you are truly balanced, your horse will be more relaxed. Learning to use your horse's "body speak" for feedback about your position will take some practice. Common sense should suggest it may not be your lack of balance that is the cause of his nervousness when he is standing at the starting line amidst eighty other horses.

The calf of your leg should rest just behind the girth and remain in contact with your horse's side. If your feet and legs are carried toward your horse's elbow, in front of your vertical line of balance, you will have less control and will be less effective at assisting your horse to carry itself properly. Your heel should be slightly lower than your toe. This position allows the greatest freedom and shock-absorbing capacity in the ankle joint. Placing the stirrup under the ball of the foot is the least tiring. Stirrup contact too close to the toe or the heel can cause sore calf muscles, numb feet and sore knees. Allowing the ankle to flex or roll outward, putting pressure on the outside edge of the foot (the little toe side) and stirrup can cause shin splints.

When trail riding, you may choose to hold the reins either in one or both hands and may ride on contact or with the reins loose, as it suits your style and your horse. Safety, control, gait, and terrain are the determining factors which should dictate your choice. You should feel comfortable switching from one way of holding the reins to the other. If your horse requires greater control, a two-handed approach is desirable. If your horse is relaxed, not traveling on its forehand or going downhill at speed, you may opt to give it complete freedom of its head and neck by riding with only one hand on the reins and with the rein fully extended. The latter method encourages the horse to stretch its head and neck forward and down, relaxing the back and increasing its stride length, especially at walk. You need to take care, however, when giving your horse a completely loose rein, that the horse doesn't loose its concentration and sleepwalk (when this happens, the horse is prone to stumbling) or become lazy and let its forehand carry the entire weight (a state referred to as *forehand-heavy*). If you usually ride with only one hand on the reins, be sure to switch hands periodically. Extending only one arm causes the torso to twist slightly, making the pressure on your horse's back from your seatbones un-even. Over lots of miles this can cause problems in your horse's back and can even alter its way of moving.

Stiff shoulders, elbows, wrists or fingers transfer tension and motion to the horse's mouth even on a loose rein, so you need to keep your arms and hands relaxed and use care when making contact with the horse through the rein. One way to increase awareness is to think about feeling what is at the other end of the rein you are holding, rather than just feeling the material (leather, biothane, rope) of the rein itself. Look for the sensations in your hand and fingers that are produced by the rein contacting the bit (metal) and the bit contacting the horse's mouth (flesh and bone). Once you have pictured this, focus on feeling it at a walk. A good rider with a tension-free body can feel all of that—as well as feeling, with their left hand, what their right hand is doing with the rein on the right side of the horse and vice versa. Developing this degree of feel ("good hands") takes practice, time, patience and the willing-ness to explore. Refusing to make contact with the horse's mouth through the reins is not the same as having good hands ("no hands" are not good hands, they are just no hands). If the rider needs to take a feel of the bit to help her horse do its job better (for instance to keep the horse gathered up and bal-anced at eighty miles while trotting down a long hill into a vet check), but has always refused to make contact with her horse's mouth in the mistaken belief she will hurt her horse by doing so, she has shortchanged and jeopardized her partner.

The photo shows a laterally unbalanced rider, with her weight on the left side of the horse's back. Notice how the stirrups of this rider appear to be uneven. In fact, they are exactly the same length, but the rider's weight has shifted the saddle to the left of center, making the right stirrup appear to be short.

◄

The rider, when viewed directly from the front or rear, should appear to sit squarely in the middle of the horse at all times. Any tendency to lean (shoulders not parallel to the ground) or drift to one side of the saddle (pants seam not lining up over the horse's spine) can sore the horse's back. Either problem will, in time, cause the horse to become unbalanced in its muscular development and build more muscles on the side on which the rider is sitting. Close attention should also be paid to the stirrups being even. A rider who sits crookedly on his or her horse's back often appears to have uneven stirrups. A crooked rider also causes the saddle to shift, again creating soring problems.

A rider positioned to "flow" with the horse without weighting its forehand unduly, as it trots down a moderate incline. ➤

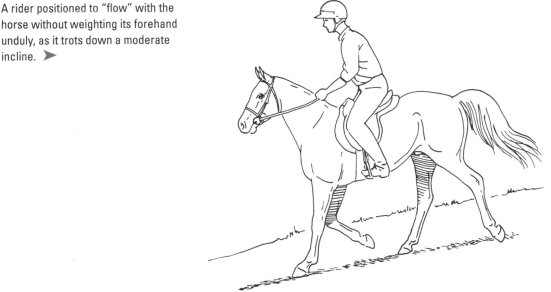

When riding either up or downhill you should insure that your weight remains off your horse's loins, allowing the horse the full use of its loins to balance itself more easily. It is not appropriate to lean back when the horse is going downhill (despite Hollywood's depiction of the downhill ride in *The Man From Snowy River*). If the uphill is exceptionally steep, use the horse's mane to help keep your torso forward. When riding downhill, keep your torso directly over your feet. You should appear as though you would drop onto your feet in a balanced crouch if the horse disappeared from between your legs. Allowing your heels to drop a bit lower than usual on a steep downhill gives you added security and helps to keep your pelvis from sliding forward against the front of the saddle (a very uncomfortable position, not only be-cause of the beating it can give you, but also because your body will want to arch backward, which will put a lot of tension in your low back during the descent). If the ascent or descent is steep, use the calf to help keep your legs and seat in the most effective and inoffensive position.

Allow your hip, knee and ankle joints to be moved by the horse when trot-ting downhill. When correct, your joints will feel as though you are jogging down the hill yourself. If you can find this sensation, your body will *float* around the horse as if in a sling formed by the stirrups and stirrup leathers, and will offer no barrier to the horse's free-forward movement. When riders allow this state by their own balance and freedom, many horses are capable of flying down even steep hills with little or no increase of concussion on their legs and feet. Indeed, they too seem to float as they roll down the hill, touch-ing the ground only briefly and very lightly. Since very little muscle or energy is being used by the horse when it is freewheeling in this manner, the heart rate will drop, sometimes dramatically, by the time it reaches the bottom of a long hill. The illusion of "stillness" that marks a good rider is gained when horse and rider are moving together in harmony, rather than when the rider is physically rigid or tense. If you fail to allow your hips, knees or ankles free movement, your horse will develop a shortened downhill stride and will be more prone to stumbling and stifle injuries.

One of the best exercises for learning how to release and re-ceive the motion of a downhill trot is to work on a minitrampoline. This device is also great for unlocking *holding* patterns (tension) in your body, enabling you to improve a host of skills, from de-veloping good hands, to following the canter, releasing the back, and eliminating back pain.

Work on the minitrampoline is an excellent way to pinpoint counterproductive holding patterns (long-standing muscular spasms) in the rider's body and release unwanted tension from the muscles.

◀

THE POSTING TROT

The posting or rising trot is often done incorrectly with too much tension in the rider's body. To post correctly, the horse must be allowed to be the activating agent of the upward and forward swing of the rider's hips. If you *lift* or push yourself out of the saddle with your own muscles, you end up pushing against your stirrups, stiffening your knees and jamming the saddle against your horse's back. Once you have vaulted into the air in this manner, the horse's momentum will overtake you and cause you to descend (fall) back into the saddle, behind the horse's forward-moving balance point.

In addition to putting you out of sync with your horse, this way of posting the trot exhibits a body posture with a lot of tension. When you land on the horse's back, you cannot control the impact of contact except by pinching the muscles of your inner thighs together—which is counterproductive because it requires excess tension in the body. This pattern of body use repeats itself over and over during a 50- or 100-mile ride. It sores the horse's back, causes lameness, early fatigue and emotional stress in the horse (sometimes in the rider too), and develops a defensive "hollowed back" posture in the horse, which in time causes the long muscles of the back to atrophy, thus contributing to saddle fit problems.

To learn to post easily and in balance with the horse, you must locate your physical hip joint. Not where you *think* it is, but where it in fact *is*, on your body.

Learning Exercise 4   Stand on one leg, and lift your other knee slightly so your foot rests on your toe. This action produces a pronounced crease in the flexed leg, where the leg joins your torso. Explore this crease from your hip to your groin with your finger. About half way between your hip and your groin, in approximately the middle of your thigh, your finger tip will pass over a ropelike ligament. Move your finger to the groin side of this ligament and point toward your pelvis. You are pointing at the spot in your body where the ball sits in the socket joint. It is from here that your upper body must be moved when you are seated in the saddle. It is also from this point that the leg finds its freedom to be used to aid and guide the horse. If the adductor muscles (grippers) on the inside of the thighs are tightened or tensed, they pinch the horse's back. If the adductor and/or gluteus maximus (buttocks) muscles are tightened, the rider will "bounce" on the horse, in the same way a rubber ball bounces away from a hard surface.

Learning Exercise 5   Once you have located your true hip joint, position yourself over a level bench or chair about the height of the back of your knees. Touch the bench with your calves so you know it is there, then look forward and sit down the way you normally do. Notice how you land. Also consider whether or not you could have prevented yourself from sitting on a tack that was quickly placed under you at the last possible second. Now get up in your usual way. As you do, observe how much pressure/tightness you put in your lower back muscles and chest (pectoral muscles) in order to rise. Now prepare to sit down again, only this time use your fingers to locate your hips. Press them backward gently while you fold your torso forward without arching your back. Having positioned your hips over the bench in this manner, stop thinking backwards and instead kneel down. Continue to kneel as you descend to the bench until you feel your butt touch down—then just allow your upper body to float to the vertical. You will notice when you do this that you landed very lightly on the bench; further, if you paid attention, you will realize that you could have changed your descent into an ascent at any point along the way, even when you felt your *pants* touch the bench.

That is balance. It is also a balanced biomechanical use of the joints in the body to lower the body over the feet. If you post by using your body in this same manner—by releasing your thighs and sliding through the knee as though you were kneeling down to your saddle—you will never run the risk of pounding your horse's kidneys with your posting. Many riders, especially men, adopt a "chair seat" to protect important parts of their anatomy. Releasing the tension in your lower back will allow your pelvis to safely take a more natural upright position. Your pubic bone and other tender parts will rise when the pelvis rights itself and will no longer come in contact with the saddle (unless the saddle you are riding is too small for you). If you use your body mechanics correctly when you post, posting will be easy to do and easy on the horse.

Posting on the Correct Diagonal

Posting with a specific diagonal set of the horse's legs as they move together at the trot is usually considered something which concerns arena riders more than trail riders. But it is just as important for the trail rider to learn to recognize the diagonal at which she is posting, and to be able to change diagonals to insure her horse develops both sides of its body equally. When the horse trots, it throws the rider's weight into the air with one hind leg or the other. If the rider is rising when the horse's right front leg swings forward, the left hind leg is the "loading" leg, or the leg which is pushing the rider's weight off the horse's back. This means the left hind leg works harder every stride than the right hind leg. The muscles that provide the power to the left hind leg become bigger and stronger.

Think of it this way: If you stuck your arm out in front of you, retracted it back to your shoulder and pushed it forward again, repeating the motion 100 times every day for a month, you would strengthen the muscles you used to do that movement. But if a friend put his or her hand against yours and resisted your efforts, making you work harder to straighten your arm, you would become twice as strong in half the time. This is called *isometric exercise* and it is a very effective way of building body strength in both a horse and rider.

If, when you condition and compete your horse, you are always rising on the same diagonal, your horse will soon be stronger on one side than the other. A horse that is one-sided in this way will use itself unevenly, creating a crooked movement pattern that stresses its body in the same way you would yours if you tried to run by taking a long stride with one leg and a short one with the other. Pretty soon all the muscles of your pelvis and torso will be torqued and tired. The next stop on this path is lameness.

To help develop your horse evenly, you must be sure you spend time posting on each diagonal. When a horse becomes one-sided he will deliberately try to keep the rider from posting on his weak hind leg.

During training and competition, a rider should change his or her posting diagonal every two to three miles to even the wear and tear on the horse and encourage equal-sided muscle development.

The easiest way to find out which diagonal you like to rise on is to simply have someone watch you rise to the trot and tell you which of your horse's front legs is swinging forward when your body is rising, or which leg is on the ground when you are sitting in the saddle. If you have never been taught to change your diagonals (or don't even know what they are), there is a good chance you will always choose and stay on a particular one. The most common method of checking your diagonal is to look down at the point of the horse's shoulder. By watching as it swings forward, you can see the diagonal with which you are rising. Taking your eyes off the trail while you try to determine the diagonal you are using may mean missing a trail marker how-ever, so it is best to learn to *feel* which diagonal you are using.

Learning Exercise 6   Picture yourself floating above your horse. You can look down and see the horse as a shadowy outline without detail. Paint a white line down the middle of the outline right where your horse's spine would be. Now paint another one across the horse just where the rider sits. Now float down into the saddle again. Pretend your shadow outline horse is on a com-puter screen. Click on the right front quarter of the outline and highlight it. Let the other three sections go dark. With this picture in your mind, let your-self become aware of any repeating sensation that you can feel in your right knee, thigh, hip, calf (if it is properly against the horse's rib cage where it belongs), or right foot where it rests on the stirrup. Once you locate a spot on your body where you can feel a specific movement over and over as the horse walks along under you, start to count out loud as you feel the movement. Have a friend watch the horse and tell you what it is doing with its right front leg each time you count. This will tell you what the sensation you are experi-encing in your body means. As soon as you know this, you have your "land-mark." For instance, let's say you can feel your right hip drop a little bit every other second. You start to count one every time you feel that feeling. Your helper or instructor watches you and tells you your horse is reaching forward with his right front leg when you feel that particular sensation in your body. Now repeat the exercise on the left side. Then try it again at the trot.

You will find with a little practice and help that you will be able to attach a meaning to the feelings you experience in specific parts of your body when the horse is trotting. By identifying the feelings and what they mean in this man-ner, you can select changes that will put you on the diagonal of your choice. To change your diagonal, all you need to do is either stay up in the air for one extra beat or stay down in the saddle for one extra beat. Some riders find it easier to do it one way and some the other. It doesn't make any difference which you choose, so choose the type of change which is easiest for you. If you practice changing under someone's watchful eye frequently for about a month, you will always be able to feel your diagonals.

Horses move by alternately moving first one side, then the other side of their body, just like humans do. In the horse, one side of the back is always rising while the other side is falling or becoming hollow. If you attempt to sit evenly on both seatbones simultaneously or to keep equal weight in both stirrups simultaneously, the motion and movement of your horse's body will oppose you. To ride that way you would need to ride a rabbit or a kangaroo— an animal who moves its hind legs forward at the same time—not a horse.

Learning Exercise 7 To let your body put a "feel" to this idea, ride your horse quietly at a walk with your feet out of the stirrups. Notice how the horse moves your body. Pay attention to specific body parts, not just your whole body in general. You will find your entire pelvis does not move forward at the same time. First your left hip is pushed forward by the horse's left hind leg acting against the ground and then your right hip is moved forward when his right hind leg thrusts. Once your hip has gotten started forward by the push from the horse's hind foot, gravity continues to take it forward, sucking your seatbones into the hollow place of the back created when the horse's rib cage descends and swings to the opposite side of his body as he moves. If you have trouble picturing this, stand behind a horse and watch its belly swing from side to side as it walks away from you.

Although pleasure or competitive trail riders are more apt than endurance riders to sit to the trot, the key to being able to sit the trot well is knowing the secret of the hollow side and letting your weight settle onto your hip on the hollow side of the horse's back, rather than trying to keep it down on the side that is struggling to come up underneath you At the walk it is easy to feel the division between the two sides of your horse's body. If you allow your horse to move you with its motion, his back muscles will feel less restricted by your weight and he will be better able to swing his legs deeper underneath him, producing a longer-strided, ground-covering walk. If you are unable to feel the different sides of your horse at walk, you are probably squeezing or gripping with your thighs. If you find this to be the case or if you suspect it might be, do the following exercise.

Learning Exercise 8 Tighten your inner thigh muscles, pressing your thighs and knees as hard against the saddle as you can for several strides. Now release that pressure and let your legs hang down the horse's sides in a relaxed manner. You can repeat this exercise several times. As you do more of what is wrong, you are building a comparison scale in your mind and body that will then allow you to notice when you do even a little bit of the undesirable action (gripping). Notice what your body feels like when you apply the pressure and what it feels like when you let that tension go. Remember doing Learning

Exercise l on the ground? Pressing your thighs and knees into the horse is just like what you did when you held your arms stiff and pressed your palms hard against your partner's sides. You can feel how the tension affects your ability to move freely and follow your horse just as it did in the ground exercise. Your horse feels it too; it affects his movement just the way it affected yours when you took your turn at being the horse during Learning Exercise 1.

RIDING THE CANTER WELL

Being able to use the two sides of your body independently is also necessary to ride canter without bouncing. The canter is a three-beat gait where the horse pushes off with the outside hind leg. When he does so, he sends energy through his body and through the rider's body as well. If the rider's body is free of tension, the horse's energy will flow through the rider, lifting the rider's hips and carrying them forward. If the rider is locked in any of his or her shock-absorbing joints (ankle, knees, or hip), or is unable to find his or her own independent two-sided motion because of tense, binding torso muscles, the energy generated from the horse's thrusting foot will propel the rider's body into space. This is what is happening when you see a rider bounce in the saddle at canter. If a rider bounces at canter it is hard on the horse. The rider's weight, once in the air, must then land on the horse's back again, producing an impact with each canter stride that ranges from mild (featherweight) to significant (heavyweight).

The first step to improving your ability to harmonize with your horse at canter, is to learn to visualize the mechanics of what is happening underneath you when you ride. Videos are a good resource to see horses in action or to study a rider's form. Notice how the horse's legs seem to make a rounder action when they canter. This is because they use their joints and back more at canter than at trot.

Did you ever pretend you were a horse when you were a kid, cantering or galloping around a room? Strange as it may seem, if you did, you were practicing riding your horse. Your ankle, knee and hip joints need to do almost the same thing for you to *ride* your horse smoothly at canter, as they did to allow you to imitate the movement of the horse when you were young.

The horse's body rises and falls during the canter and its barrel swings from one side to the other, just like at trot and walk. When relaxed and tension-free, your legs, which lay over the horse's barrel, will be lifted and dropped alternately as the horse moves forward in canter. This lifting and dropping of the leg only happens if you allow your hip joints to be folded up and then opened up again by the motion of the horse. The opening and closing of the joints on your right and left sides will closely follow each other, but do not happen together.

Think of riding your horse's back as you would a surfboard.

Allow the energy of your horse's canter to lift your hips and carry them forward as though you were riding a surfboard on a wave. ▶

When the wave of the horse's energy lifts you, you must keep your knees bent and use your ankle joints to follow that energy as it moves you and your board (saddle) forward. If you lock your hips, you get left behind the motion and fall off your board backward. If you stiffen your knees or ankles you can't absorb the lateral motion of the board and you tumble off sideways. Many of the same dynamics of motion and gravity that affect surfers and skiers also affect riders. When you ride, however, if you lack balance, you can grip the horse with your muscles and fool yourself into thinking you are doing well because you are staying on. Because you can't grip skis or surfboards, if you stiffen and lose your ability to balance in those sports, you fall.

A classic way to become better at riding the canter is to be lunged without stirrups. To do this you need the assistance of a good instructor or a friend who knows how to lunge a horse correctly (keep them in a stable rhythm at the end of a lunge line) and a horse who will move into canter smoothly and stay in a steady rhythm on the circle. Endurance horses are not noted for being good at such things. If you ask them to perform a smooth, steady canter on a large circle in an arena, many lean in and quicken, especially if the circle is smaller than 20 meters wide. Lungeing will only benefit you if the horse you use is able to give a steady, balanced canter for a long enough period of time to allow you to sort out the tension in your body, release it, and get the feel of your body moving with the horse *without tension*. This concept is often expressed in equestrian books as the rider "finding his or her seat." If the horse being lunged is unbalanced, your internal gyroscope will alert your brain and you will contract your muscles in an unconscious attempt to prevent the fall which your brain is sure is coming. It is impossible for even the most diligent student to find any significant release in body tension in this scenario, no matter how long he or she spends going around and around in a circle on the lunge line. Any gripping action of your legs or thighs will prevent your hips from moving with the horse's back. Grip will keep you on, but it prevents harmony and interferes with the efficient, relaxed, muscular actions that produce the ground-covering stride of a good endurance horse.

Many riders either grip their horse with their thighs to keep their seat from bouncing at canter or else they stand in their stirrups. They know that bouncing on the horse's back is not good for the horse, but they do not know how to release their joints so they can sit without bouncing. The intent in this approach to the problem is good but the mechanics of execution are faulty. If a rider grips with her thighs to keep her seat light, she is limiting her horse's freedom to use its body and to defend its soundness by moving lightly over the ground. If the rider stands, using her stirrups rather than her thigh muscles to keep her above her horse's back when it canters, her weight is transferred in full force to the saddle tree and again, the horse's ability to move freely is impaired by too great a concentration of the rider's weight right behind its shoulder.

Learning Exercise 9   A great way to help find and unlock your hip joints while unmounted is to use a physioball, a ball about 2 1/2 to 3 feet tall. Sit on it with both feet on the floor, (your pelvis and thigh bones forming a V). Now try to make the ball track around two perfect circles which touch in the middle at the center, like a figure eight. Push the ball forward to begin the circles, first to the right and then to the left. Maneuver the ball with your hips, controlling the direction of the line with the muscles of your back and pelvis. Don't push with your feet, just allow them to stabilize you as you attempt to control and release your back muscles and hip joints in the coordinated way it takes to do the exercise. It sounds easy, but in order to make the ball track in a perfect circle in each direction, you will have to release *all* tension in *each* hip joint and be flexible in your lower back. It's a challenging exercise. For feedback, watch yourself in a mirror to see if you are really making perfectly round circles.

> *Shallow breathing is a cause of tension in the body. A rider needs to breathe efficiently when working. Holding your breath during a tense moment is normal, but some riders hold their breath a little bit all the time by simply not breathing deeply. It's not surprising that holding your breath causes tension, because if you don't breathe, you will die within minutes and your brain knows it. Any tension in the rider communicates itself to the horse and significantly reduces the rider's ability to ride in balance, think clearly, and react quickly. Observe your breathing pattern in a quiet setting. If you do not breathe deeply when you are relaxed, you most certainly will not breathe deeply when you are excited. Focus on inhaling fully when you breathe, especially if you are nervous or overly tense. It will help you remain relaxed and make you better able to cope with what is happening.*

RIDING TURNS

A horse can execute a bending line (turn) in one of two ways: He can go through the turn (1) like a motorcycle or (2) like a train.

If he goes through the corner without bending his body, he is like a motorcycle and must lean in as he goes through the turn. This is the most natural way for the horse to turn, and is the way he does it when he is not being ridden. When the horse is carrying a rider, we want him to negotiate turns more like a train than a motorcycle. A train remains level through a turn; its outside wheels don't come off the tracks.

A motorcycle must lean in a turn because it can not bend.

A train executes a turn in a level manner, making it more stable.

There are four important reasons why we want the horse to mimic a train by flexing his body laterally and remaining balanced over all four of his legs, rather than leaning like a motorcycle on the inner two:

1. Safety.   If the horse is leaning in the curve, he is putting his inside hind leg toward his belly button when it lands, giving himself more of an ice-skate base than a roller-skate base. This narrowing of the hind legs destabilizes his hind end, causing his hips to become unlevel. In this leaning posture, if his inside foot should hit a slick spot (moisture, dried leaves, slate rock), he is much more likely to loose his balance and fall than he would be if his hind legs were spread, enabling the inside leg to act as a brace against the pull of gravity.

An unbalanced turn to the left. The horse's body is bent away from the direction of the turn and its left front leg and shoulder bear most of its weight. Photo: Pat Mitchell. ➤

Both horse and rider exhibit good balance on this turn. Both are looking in the direction of the turn, and the rider's body is balanced over the column of her inside leg. Photo: Pat Mitchell.

◄

2. Control.   A horse who is unstable in its hind end will not be able to balance itself comfortably over its hind legs. This means it will, of necessity, have to keep most of its weight on its forehand. The forehand-heavy horse is not only harder to steer, but is less responsive. Unlike a balanced horse, it is simply unable to respond promptly to the rider's signals to slow, stop or turn. When the finish line at a major event is off a turn, and first place is decided between two front-running horses by no more than a neck—believe me—you will want a

horse who is responsive. The inside route (and the difference between first and second place) through that turn is twenty-five feet shorter than the outside line. The horse that can respond to its rider's rein aids the quickest will be the one that gets that inside line for those last few yards.

3. Soundness. When the horse leans his body heavily to one side and angles his legs toward his centerline, his inside legs take more of the concussion. The hoof comes in contact with the ground at an angle rather than landing level, so the concussion passes up the joints unevenly, compressing one side of the joint a great deal. This predisposes the horse to early injury, strain and eventual structural breakdown.

4. Comfort. Cantering an unbalanced horse through a sharp turn is a scary feeling. Only if you are a very good rider will you be able to keep from gripping when your internal gyroscope sends a "tilt" signal to your brain telling it both you and your horse are about to come crashing to the ground sideways.

In order for the horse to maintain or regain his balance in the turn and flow through it freely, the rider must be able to (1) maintain her lateral balance by keeping her inside hip over her turning foot, just as she would if she were making a turn on the ground, and (2) position her body to match her horse's body during the turn.

Learning Exercise 10   Position yourself in front of a mirror, in a riding stance with your feet spread and your knees bent. Now turn your torso to the left as you pretend to ride a turn in that direction. Think you're balanced? Can you raise your right foot off the floor, resting it lightly on the toe? Did you have to move more of your weight over your right leg in order to do that? If you did, you would not have been in balance with your horse on the turn.

Since the horse is long from nose to tail, when he is correctly curved on a circle, his shoulders and his hips do not form a parallel line, but instead form lines that would meet at the center of the bend if it was extended into a circle. As rider, you need to do the exact same thing by bringing your inside shoulder up and back slightly, letting your outside shoulder swing forward. This positions your torso so that your collar bones form a parallel line with your horse's shoulders. If you imagine a set of automobile headlights emanating from the

Marie demonstrates the correct body position for riding a turn to the left. Photo: Donna Snyder-Smith.

Marie is practicing the turning exercise incorrectly, allowing her weight to stay on her right foot as she positions herself to turn her horse to the left with her upper body and the reins.

Marie is now following through correctly in the left turn, keeping her hip aligned over her turning leg as she rotates her shoulders, and looking in the direction her horse is traveling.

rider's front, you would see that by swinging his or her shoulders in the above manner, the beams from these headlights would shine directly down the middle of the road, or curving line.

The rider's hips need to form a parallel line with the horse's hips as well. This happens if you draw your inside foot a little toward the horse's stifle and lower your inside knee toward the ground as though preparing to kneel on the inside knee. Another way to accomplish the correct biomechanical action is to "ground your inside foot" by reaching directly downward, letting the knee drop *slightly* away from the saddle, and imagining yourself putting your foot flat on the ground. This action, when correctly executed, accomplishes a number of results:

1. It causes your inside seat bone to be drawn forward.

2. It causes your inside calf to rest against the horse's rib cage in the area of the girth, forming the "bending leg" or post around which the horse curves its body.

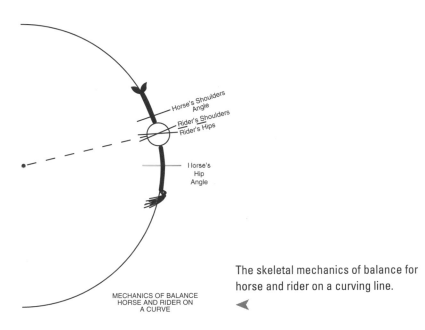

The skeletal mechanics of balance for horse and rider on a curving line.

3. It makes your hips form a parallel line with your horse's hips, and completes the match of your body position to your horse's body position.

Drawing the outside leg behind the girth helps insure that your inside hip stays forward, and puts your outside leg in a position to create one wall of the channel through which the horse's energy is directed. Now you and your horse are one, and your horse is free to use its muscles to move forward rather than having to use them to counterbalance you on its back.

Learning Exercise 11   Grab the right arm of a friend and pretend he or she is your horse. With arms linked, walk toward a spot in the room together side by side. When you get there, tell your horse to turn away from you to its left. Your "horse" must try as hard as it can to obey the imaginary signals you are giving it to turn with the left rein.

While your horse is trying to obey your instructions and make the turn to the left, lean your body to the right. Although your linked arms will keep you from flying off and your "horse" will drag you through the turn if he or she is strong enough, the entire experience will be unpleasant for both of you. The amount of extra effort your horse needs to use to obey your command to turn

If the rider fails to keep his weight over his inside leg when asking/riding a turn, it causes the horse to have to work much harder to accomplish the maneuver. ➤

left should be obvious to you. Now do the exercise again, only this time use your body to mirror your "horse" partner's body by keeping your shoulders touching during the entire turn. What happened? Neither of you leaned at all and the turn was accomplished in a smooth flowing manner with almost no effort.

On your real horse, you will find it takes very little pressure from the reins to accomplish a turn in this manner. What it all boils down to is this: When you are unbalanced, with your weight in the outside stirrup coming into or going through a turn, your horse is forced to lock its body into a tense counterbalancing position. This tense position puts lots of stress on the joints of the horse (the faster the pace, the greater the stress), and wastes the horse's energy, keeping it from using itself efficiently during a ride. It also unbalances the horse's shoulders, causing it to lean in its turns.

If your horse leans on turns, you'd better put on barrel racing kneepads if you ride a knee-knocker trail (a narrow trail that snakes in and out of closely growing trees). If, on the other hand, you and your horse are balanced and working as a team in the quickly changing turns, you can whip through that type of trail, leaving your competition eating your dust while they wonder how you escaped with your kneecaps still attached to your legs.

COMMON POSITION PROBLEMS, EFFECTS AND CORRECTIONS

The Curl

Symptoms   The rider collapses in the rib cage, compressing one side of his or her body. The head is sometimes carried tilted. The shoulders become tilted; the shoulder on the contracted side usually being the one closer to the ground. The rider sits with more weight on one side of the saddle, pressing that seatbone down into the horse's back. The rider's leg on the inside of the curl feels and looks shorter than the other leg. When observed from the front, the collapsed rider appears to have uneven stirrups.

The rider with a contracted side "curls" her body in the direction of the contraction. This causes the rider to distribute her weight unevenly on the horse's back. The rider may have trouble making a solid connection with the stirrup on the side opposite the curl.

Effects   The rider's crooked posture causes the horse to travel crookedly. A crooked use of the body increases stress on joints, tendons and ligaments, increasing the chance of injury. Riding crooked can also sore the horse's back, because the saddle will follow the rider's reaching leg, working its way off center toward the rider's long leg side.

Solution   Tickle a cloud—stretch the arm on your collapsed side over your head and wiggle your fingers until you feel your pelvis become level. Check to make sure your stirrups are even by using a tape measure. *Do not guess, measure!* Correct them if you find they are uneven. If you continue to feel as though your stirrups are uneven once you have made sure they are correct by measuring them, it is a sign *you* are sitting crooked. Move your hips directly toward the stirrup that feels the shortest. Use the hand over your head exercise as often as necessary, carrying it up for a few strides, then letting it drop and putting it back up again, until your body begins to form a new map that allows your shoulders and hips to be carried level.

Having the toe in a position that is lower than the heel when making contact with the stirrup is guaranteed to freeze/stiffen the ankle, preventing it from doing its job as an important part of the rider's shock-absorbing system. ➤

Stiff Ankles/Toe Below Heel

Symptoms   The joints of the rider's leg are stiff, and the ankle is unable to fulfill its role as a major shock absorber. The rider makes contact with the stirrup by pushing the toe down or pushing the ball of their foot against the stirrup with a raised heel. The stiff leg then prevents the rider from centering her body so she can move with her horse without effort.

Effects   The lack of shock-absorbing capacity in the joints of the rider's leg due to a stiffened ankle joint—or pressure against the stirrup that stiffens the ankle joint—will cause the rider to grip and bounce. A rider using tension to grip her horse restricts the horse from using his body to move in balance. This decreased freedom of movement in the horse causes increased wear and tear on its limbs and back over the miles/years of competition. Pressure against the stirrup can cause the rider numb feet. If the ankle is rolled outward or "rounded" while the foot is receiving pressure, it can cause pain in the ankle and shin-splints.

Solutions Unmounted   (1) Get a 2 × 4 board about 3 feet long. Place it on a level surface. Put the balls of your feet up on the board with your heels on the ground/floor, your legs a hip-width apart, and your knees slightly bent as though you are riding your horse.

A simple 2 × 4 board is an easy way to map the correct feeling of the function of the ankles and feet when they are placed in the stirrup in a mechanically advantageous way.

◄

Roll your knees toward each other slightly until the weight on your foot where it is in contact with the board is evenly distributed from the big toe side to the little toe side. Do a very gentle bounce in your ankles with your feet in this position. Spend 10 minutes a day with your feet in this position if it does not cause you any discomfort, teaching your body the correct feel (body map) for your foot position in the stirrup. If the muscles or tendons in the back of your legs, shins or elsewhere are too tight to allow you to do this comfortably with a 2 × 4, reduce the thickness of the board and work up. (2) Assume a stretched position by placing your palms against a wall and walking your feet backward until you are leaning toward the wall, supported by your hands.

Keep your feet flat on the floor. Also, keep your back flat, not arched. When you step out of the exercise do so by advancing one leg forward toward the wall and take your weight on that leg as you straighten your body.

This exercise, known as the skier's stretch, is designed to lengthen the Achilles tendons, making the ankle more flexible.

◄

By pushing down on the toe against the stirrup, the rider . . .

. . . pushes herself up out of the saddle, then releases the downward pressure on the toe—and without sitting down in the saddle again . . .

. . . allows her ankle to relax, settling her heel into a position that is slightly lower than her toe.

Mounted exercises   (1) Push yourself up on tiptoe against your stirrups, extending your toe downward like a ballet dancer does, as far as you can. This will push your body up away from the saddle. Hold that extended position for the count of ten, then release the tension in your ankle and allow your heel and leg to sink down toward the ground. Do not actually sit in the saddle. Repeat this exercise three times before beginning to ride. Body-map the feel of the released ankle with your heel lower than your toe. (2) Scrunch your toes up in your boot, holding them as tightly compressed as you can while you count to ten. Now spread your toes out and wiggle them. You will notice your ankle release as you release the tightness in your toes. (3) With your feet out of the stirrups and your legs hanging against your horse's rib cage, try to draw perfect circles with your foot. Pretend you have a pencil stuck in the toe of your boot and there is a pad of paper in front of the pencil. The roundness (range of motion) of the circle is more important than its size. Make the circles in both a clockwise and counterclockwise direction. Do one foot at a time so you can pay attention to what your foot is doing.

Tension In Upper Body

Symptoms   The rider's torso and hip joints are locked with tension. The rider appears stiff and her hands tend to be unsteady, sometimes pulling on the reins. The rider's jaw may also be clenched. When the horse initiates an increase in forward energy, especially if the rider doesn't expect it, the rider's upper body experiences a whiplash response, her shoulders falling behind the vertical line for a moment until she can regain her equilibrium.

Effects   Any tension is detrimental to the harmony of horse and rider. A stiff rider is a passenger, not a partner. Imagine a beautifully dressed woman on a dance floor. Her gown is gorgeous, her hair is perfect and she is so tense she feels like a piece of waterlogged wood to her partner who has to drag her around. She may be moving her legs, but the flow that is necessary to produce an attractive picture for the observer is missing. Tension in a rider's upper body is often the cause of backaches and sore shoulder muscles during and after a ride. It can also cause headaches and light-headedness.

Solutions unmounted   (1) Working on the small trampoline is an excellent way to break up tension and detrimental holding patterns in the upper body of the rider. (2) The shoulder shrug is also helpful in releasing tension. Simply pull your shoulders forward and up around your ears as high and as tightly as you can possibly get them.
  The more you scrunch them up around your ears, the better. Hold them there for ten strides, then let them drop quickly and shake them out like a dog shaking water off its coat. Caution: Remember to breathe while holding the shoulders tightly and *do not* lift your chin as you lift your shoulder.

The shoulder shrug is an easy way for the rider to help eliminate destructive tension from the upper back, neck and shoulder area.
◄

The Hook Leg

Symptoms   The rider is laterally crooked in the saddle when viewed from behind. The toe on the leg she hooks around the horse to stabilize herself points directly outward because her heel and the back of her calf are pulled against the horse continuously. The knee on the hook leg is further away from the saddle than the knee on the other side. Her other leg lays nicely against the saddle with the ankle and toe relaxed in a normal position. A rider with a hook leg may also exhibit a curl, leaning toward her hooking leg, but this is not always the case.

Effects   Since the rider is riding in a crooked manner, the horse's ability to move straight is also compromised. If the rider is curling, or unleveling her shoulders, she will be placing almost all the stress of her weight on only one side of her horse's back. If she allows her opposite foot to move in front of the girth, bracing it against the stirrup, she will twist her torso as she posts, moving her body forward on the diagonal instead of keeping her spine in line with the spine of her horse as she rises. The hook leg can stress the rider's hip joints and make them sore—especially the one on the side where the leg is hooked, since it is taking most of the stress. Backaches and between-the-shoulders aches can also occur as a result of the constantly twisting torso during miles and miles of posting trot.

Solution Mounted   Standing still, slip your hand, palm upward, between your saddle and your thigh from behind the leg.

In this exercise the rider lifts her thigh and rotates the inner muscles towards the back of the saddle with her hand, also rotating the ball in the socket joint so the leg/hip juncture becomes wider and the leg can lay in a relaxed manner on the side of the saddle without pinching. Keeping the opposite hand over the head while doing this helps keep the rider from tipping her body forward and taking her seatbones and buttocks out of saddle contact. ➤

Grasp a piece of your pants or the muscle of your thigh and pull it toward the rear with you as you slide your hand back out from under your leg. Keep your opposite hand raised over your head. Do not tip your pelvis forward, lifting your buttocks off the saddle.

Doing this exercise will place the thigh flat against the saddle as it rotates the ball in the socket joint. It releases the hook leg, allowing the calf to make contact with the horse's ribs on its flat interior surface rather than at the back of the leg.

Pinched Knees or Gripping Thighs

Symptoms   (1) The rider's seat is leaving the saddle at canter. (2) A double bounce action occurs in the rider's seat when he or she tries to touch down on the saddle during the rising trot. (3) The rider's seat is wedged against the cantle of the saddle.

Effects   This problem causes tension in the horse's back, and can cause the horse to hollow its back under the rider. Over a period of time, this hollowing will cause the muscles of the horse's back to weaken and atrophy producing a false swaybacked appearance in the horse.

Some riders think the hollowed back appearance of some endurance horses is due to a loss of fat from the back during a campaign season. A horse that puts on weight during the winter may lose that same weight during its performance season, but muscle does not melt away with miles. When muscled up through correct development, the horse's back will not change significantly from the beginning to the end of a ride season. If your horse is experiencing this problem, add gymnastic exercises to your training to build the muscles in the region of his back and loin. Muscle-building will also cut down on saddle fit problems. Sensitive breeds, such as the Arabian, can exhibit erratic emotional behavior if uncomfortable in the area of the back. Other behaviors include hyperactivity when ridden, and an unwillingness to stand still while mounted.

Solutions   (1) Test the flexibility of your hip joints by sitting in a chair that is low enough to allow you to place your right foot flat on the ground while keeping your lower leg vertical (parallel to the chair leg).

A simple test to see how flexible you
are in the hip joint. ➤

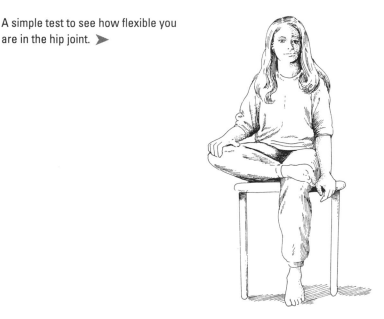

Now cross your left leg by placing it on top of your right leg with the ankle
of the crossed leg, supported above the knee of the foot that is on the floor. If
your hips are flexible enough to allow the shin bone of your crossed leg to be
parallel with the ground, you have good flexibility. If the knee of the crossed
leg points toward the ceiling instead, the tendons, ligaments and muscles around
your hip joints are tight and will need some work. When you've done this
with one leg, change and do the same thing with the other leg to test that hip
as well. To improve flexibility, sit on the ground with the bottoms of your feet
together.

Hold your ankles, feet or lower calves and gently draw your heels along the
floor toward you, keeping the soles of your feet together. This will cause your
knees to point in different directions. Fold your body forward, over your legs.
Don't force your legs open, just allow gravity to work on stretching the muscles,
tendons and ligaments around your hip area as you hold the position for as
long as is comfortable. (2) In the saddle, remove both your feet from the stirrups, and while the horse is standing still or walking slowly, lock your knees
and swing the right leg backward from the hip joint as if you were trying to
put your thigh behind the flap of the saddle. At the same time, let your left leg
swing forward past the point of the horse's shoulder. Then reverse the swing,
drawing the left leg back and letting the right leg swing forward. This is called

An exercise to open the area of the groin around the hip joint and increase hip flexibility.

◄

the scissors exercise. Be sure to move the leg from your hip joint and not from the knee. If you feel a cramp in the hip area, stop the exercise for a bit and jiggle or shake the leg loose again.

Stirrups Too Long

Symptoms The rider's leg is almost straight, with little or no flexion in the knee and ankle, thus reducing their shock-absorbing capacities. If the rider needs to move her torso into a forward position for any reason, she will round her back, thus putting a lot of strain on it. The rider's toe is forced to point down toward the ground.

Effects The rider sits more heavily in the seat, as the stirrups are not short enough to act as a part of the support frame for the rider's weight. A rounded back appearance is common in riders with long stirrups. It is also common to push the leg forward in an attempt to push the foot deeper into the stirrup. This puts the rider into what is commonly known as a chair seat, behind the balance point of her horse.

A stirrup that is too long offers no base from which the rider can take support for the upper body. This invites overuse, spasms and pain in the muscles of the lower and middle back when riding at speed or on hills. ➤

Solution   Remove your feet from the stirrups and let them hang freely down the horse's sides. Shorten the stirrups until the bottom of the stirrup hits your leg between your ankle and one inch above the sole of your foot.

What you will take from this chapter depends on your goals. You can sit on a horse, face forward, and consider yourself a rider, in the same way you can face a partner, gyrate to music and be said to be dancing. Synchronized, fluid teamwork, such as that performed by Championship Ballroom Dancing couples, requires effort, training, mental concentration and practice. To elevate dance or riding to an art form requires self-sacrifice, the will to overcome seemingly insurmountable obstacles, patience and even *more* practice! Your personal goals will be your guide to what you use and how diligently you practice what is offered in this chapter.

GYMNASTIC DEVELOPMENT OF THE ENDURANCE HORSE

Although humans have been riding horses long distances since the days of Alexander the Great, endurance riding as a sport is relatively new when compared to other equestrian disciplines such as dressage and jumping. Most historical written instruction on improving or enhancing the capabilities of the horse to travel long distances is military in nature. The most current of these military writings are the instruction manuals of the U.S. Cavalry School, at Fort Riley, Kansas, published in 1942. With little written documentation on the subject, riders have had to learn as they go which methods of training produce the best end product. For that reason, many endurance horses function at sixty percent or less of their full athletic capability. Even winning horses (with one or two exceptions), are only using about eighty percent of their ability. The primary reason for this is simple: Endurance riders think of *conditioning* when they think of training. In fact, conditioning and training are two different venues. *Both* need to be present in order for the endurance horse to reach its full performance potential.

Conditioning, which all riders do, addresses the horse's overall fitness and metabolic functions, and is as much a necessary part of the sport as the horse. *Training* (as opposed to conditioning) is what is most neglected or minimized in endurance. Training deals with the horse's efficiency, improving the biomechanical use of its body, developing strength in and balance between necessary muscle groups, and insuring a mental state suited to successful performance. In training, the rider

- balances the horse psychologically
- increases the horse's power
- increases the horse's stride length
- improves the horse's weight-carrying capacity
- develops the horse's athleticism

In this often-neglected aspect of endurance preparation lies a fifteen to forty percent edge that can put a horse ahead of the competition—both in the short term (at a finish line) and in the long term (soundness over years of performance).

A horse moving in a balanced frame with elevated back and rounded topline.
◄

An unbalanced horse, showing a hollow back, inverted neck and a shortened stride as a result of its poor biomechanical posture. ►

WHAT CONSTITUTES BALANCE IN THE HORSE?

In order to better understand the dynamics of balance and how they affect the distance riding horse, we need to understand that balance is not just a matter of whether the horse is standing up or—having stumbled—is on its knees. A horse is balanced when it has developed the necessary muscles and physical posture (or self-carriage) to facilitate distributing and supporting its own weight and the weight of its rider evenly throughout all four of its structural supports (legs, feet, etc.), both at rest and in motion. The question of balance in the horse applies both laterally and longitudinally.

A horse that lacks balance

- *Uses excess energy to accomplish the job at hand*

- *Is harder to control and steer*

- *Is more apt to stumble and fall*

- *Is subject to short-term injury (interference wounds, stone bruises, muscle sprains, tendon and ligament damage)*

- *Reduces its competitive life span by unduly stressing its skeletal structure*

- *Is less comfortable to ride*

Balance equals efficiency because it requires more energy to regain balance once it is lost than to maintain it. If you doubt this, walk across a room and notice how little effort it takes to cover the distance. Now walk across the room again. As you do, have someone approach you from behind and give you an unexpected shove, hard enough to cause you to lose your balance. How violently did your body have to react to regain its equilibrium once it had been disturbed? It took a lot of energy and muscular effort, didn't it? It also altered the fluidity of your stride, shortening it perhaps, or even causing you to stumble. You also were distracted from your focus on the task at hand. Your horse is subject to these same experiences when not traveling in balance.

In order to travel in balance with a rider, a horse needs to get its hind legs under its body where they can be used to support its weight and the weight of the rider. A horse does not engage its hind legs naturally except in those isolated moments when it is extremely animated or displaying aggression. Instead, the horse uses its hind legs predominately to propel itself, while it uses its front legs to carry itself. This system works fine when the horse is not carrying the weight of a rider on its back, but when those dynamics change, the horse's natural method of movement is no longer adequate to protect it from injury.

If you want your horse to balance itself and carry more weight on its hind legs, you must realize that the horse needs to lift or round its back to do so. The rainbow posture (also known as a rounded outline) is the first step toward balance and begins with the muscles of the abdomen. Getting the horse to contract its abdomen muscles and lift its back is not as difficult as you might imagine. If you stimulate your horse's sides below the widest part of its rib cage (some riders do it with their heels), a horse will normally respond by contracting those muscles. As the abdominal muscles contract, they lift the horse's belly and, above it, the back. One thing that might prevent this desired response is a pinching saddle that causes the horse discomfort when it lifts its back.

After the horse has raised its back, its stifle joint is free to engage the legs under the body and the legs have more room to swing under the horse's belly. This posture gives a horse greater length of stride, enabling him to cover ground more efficiently. To put his leg well under his body, the horse flexes the joints of its hind limbs. This flexion of the joints and engagement of the hind leg deeper under the body also causes his hind end to become lower. That in turn causes the shoulders to rise, meaning his front end becomes lighter and more easily directed by the rider, with his front legs and feet taking less weight on impact. It is easy to understand if you think of the horse as a seesaw. When one end goes down, the other end goes up. In the case of an endurance horse, the front end should be *up*, because a horse required by its sport to cover thousands of miles in its competitive lifetime needs to be able to move in a way that allows it to put its front feet down lightly instead of crashing down on them at every step.

Once taught to the horse by the rider, this efficient pattern of muscle use is then maintained by the rider through the coordinated use of aids, until eventually it becomes a habitual response in the horse. Gymnastic exercises help the horse strengthen the correct muscles, allowing it to spend as much time as possible using an efficient rather than a destructive posture.

When considering the question of balance in the horse, you must also consider *straightness*. Straightness equals power, and in the horse it means the ability to use both sides of the body with equal suppleness and strength. If the long-distance equine athlete is not straightened as he is conditioned, he develops a strong and a weak side. The division between the two sides becomes more pronounced the longer the horse is in training. If one hind leg is strong and pushes the horse forward with a certain amount of strength, while the other hind leg is less strong and pushes the horse forward with a lesser amount of strength, the horse's body is thrown into a constant state of compensation (tension), in order to travel in a straight line. In competition, especially if pushed to the limits of its conditioning, the horse wears out the stronger side of his body (since that is the side he will use the most) and is then forced to load his weight onto his weak side. When this happens, structural breakdown results.

During training, the rider's job is to teach the horse to respond to the rider's leg aids by: (1) lifting its belly and maintaining a rainbow frame while moving, (2) keeping its body straight, and, (3) going forward any time and in the exact amount requested. The horse learns to respond to hand and rein aids by: (1) giving to the pressure of the bit, and (2) transferring its weight onto its hind limbs as it matures and gains in strength. Once learned, these responses allow the rider to turn, stop and balance her horse as she chooses in order to best prepare her horse for the job at hand.

Once you have mastered the control of your horse, you need to put the horse through a series of gymnastic exercises designed to increase flexibility, suppleness and strength. These exercises are sometimes called *dressage*. Dressage in its pure form is a systematic, gymnastic training program perfected over hundreds of years to enable horses to perform to the limits of their athletic capabilities without injury. It should not be confused with the competition of the same name.

Ground School for the Trail and Endurance Horse

Before you mount, there are several things you can do to help your horse understand and pattern an efficient combination of motion muscles. The first is a simple neck stretch, which teaches the horse to lower its head toward the ground by relaxing and stretching the muscles along the top of its neck. Since the neck is attached to the horse's back, when the horse lowers its neck in this manner, it also stretches the muscles of his back under the saddle, causing his back to rise or come up. There is an additional little-known benefit of getting your horse to carry its head in this position—it has a calming effect on a horse's emotional state. The longer your horse can be persuaded to carry its poll at or slightly below its withers height (whether the horse is standing still or in motion), the calmer your horse will be. This is true only if the horse's *entire neck* is at this height, but does not apply if the horse's neck is arched with only its *head* held below the level of the top of its shoulder.

Thirty years of study have led to a theory about why this happens. Being a prey animal and a grazer, the horse lowers its head to eat only when it feels safe. Lowering the head in the extended-neck, grazing manner must signal the horse's body to shut off the production of any unnecessary chemicals, such as adrenaline, and focus on the digestive process instead. On the other hand, when a horse is frightened or threatened, it throws its head high in the air to get a better view of its surroundings. In this position it is ready to flee or fight. The body-language message to the brain increases adrenaline production to prepare the horse for a burst of physical activity. I have seen the following two neck-stretching exercises influence a horse's mental state to such a degree as to seem almost magical and I recommend their incorporation in the preparation and training of endurance horses.

Exercise 1   This exercise teaches the horse to lower its head on command, both from the ground and from the saddle.

Position yourself in front of the horse, making sure the horse is balanced and will not walk forward and step on you. Lower your body and induce the horse to come to you with its nose. When first trying this, you can encourage the behavior you want with some grain. As the horse lowers its head, gently tug downward on the lead rope. Release the pressure on the rope for a few seconds *every time* the horse lowers its head in response to the pressure. Eventually, the horse must follow the pull of the rope until its nose is touching the ground. It must also be willing to hold that position until you release your cue and allow it to again raise its head. To successfully train this behavior, you need to realize all horses put their heads down sometimes: to drink, to graze, and to scratch behind an ear. Your horse is "trained" *only* when it puts its head in this lowered position when *you* ask for the behavior—and *keeps* it there when it *doesn't* want to!

Teaching the horse to lower its head from the pressure in the area of the poll. ➤

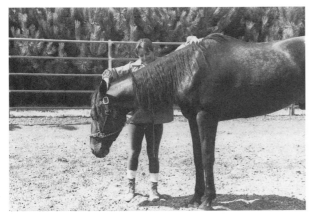

Here, the horse drops its head down willingly from a hand cue on the neck only. ➤

Asking the horse to lower its head from a gentle pull on the lead line.

Two pressure cues are combined and used simultaneously while training the horse to transfer the head-lowering response to a neck cue.

◄

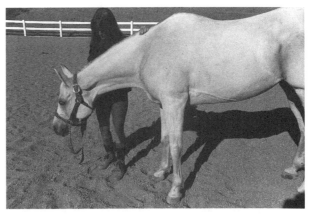

Once mounted, the rider can use the neck cue to lower her horse's head from the saddle.

◄

Now stand beside the horse, and use the same downward pressure signal on the lead rope as before, while simultaneously adding pressure with your other hand on the top of the horse's head in the area of the poll (just between the ears). Release the pressure the instant the horse moves its head downward, and repeat until the horse drops its head to the ground from your finger pressure on its poll area alone, without any cue from the lead rope. If the horse resists your finger pressure on its poll by raising its head or moving it sideways away from you, keep your fingers in the same spot and continue your cue or, failing that, bring the horse's head back into position with the lead rope and begin again. Repeat the process until the horse's head drops like a stone with just the lightest touch and stays down until you take your hand away. This could take a week or longer to train. Once the horse does the behavior, repeat it every day until it becomes an *ingrained response* and not just a choice. If you fail to make any step of this process a habitual response, when the horse is put under stress it will choose not to do the behavior!

Now ask the horse to drop its head from your touch on its poll, but as you do, pick a spot on the horse's neck (which can be reached from the saddle), and apply pressure there simultaneously. Coordinate both cues starting and stopping them together. Gradually lessen the cue near the poll, only increasing it if the horse fails to respond to your cue hand near its withers. Repeat this step until it is *habit!* Now you are ready to ask the horse to lower its head from only one hand placed close to the withers. When the horse willingly performs this step, your next step is to mount up and apply the pressure cue in the same spot on the neck near the withers, asking your horse to lower its head while you are in the saddle. If you meet resistance to this final step, have a friend help you by adding a pressure cue to your horse's head at the poll area while you cue your horse from the saddle. Repeat this saddle cue training until the horse again drops its head instantly when you touch the cue spot near the withers and *keeps its head down* until you release it by removing your hand. This behavior when cued from the saddle can

- help calm the horse during a mounted check or when you want it to stand still for some reason and it is excited.

- encourage the horse to lower its head and drink.

- discourage the horse from raising its head when it climbs a hill.

- help a horse lower its head and look at an object instead of spooking away from it.

The chambon, applied and ready to be activated by being attached to the rings of the snaffle bit. ➤

While moving at a relaxed trot on the lunge line, this 7-year-old gelding is not using his body efficiently in this frame.
◀

The same horse being lunged with the chambon in place. Notice the dip in front of the withers and the bulge on the underside of the neck have disappeared, and the muscles over the loin area are expanded and in use now. ➤

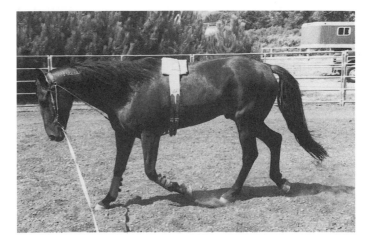

Once you discover and accomplish this handy tool, you will find endless uses for it.

You also want the horse to learn to carry its neck in a relaxed position when in motion. This can be taught before the horse is mounted by means of a training device called a *chambon*. The chambon is a simple device comprised of rope lines that fasten to the bit, run up each side of the horse's head, and pass through small rings on a leather headpiece that is attached over the poll area to the crownpiece of the bridle, and then down to a strap that passes between the horse's front legs and attaches to the girth. Shortening the lines puts pressure on the horse's poll (the chambon should only be used with a snaffle) and the corners of the horse's mouth. As soon as the horse lowers his head, all pressure exerted by the device is immediately released. It is effective because it rewards the horse for *lowering his head from his withers,* rather than for curling his neck and putting his nose on his chest). Used correctly, it does not block the free-forward extension of the horse's nose in any way. It is important to realize that in creating the rainbow frame in the horse, the entire body must exhibit the frame and not just the neck of the horse. Overbending a horse in the neck by pulling or forcing its nose in toward its chest invites several potentially severe problems, including being behind the bit and staying on the forehand.

There are some rules, however, that must be followed in the chambon's use for you and your horse to benefit from it without a risk. First, you *must* teach your horse to lower its head from poll pressure, as explained in the previous exercise. If you do not do this, your horse may react in a negative way when you hook the chambon lines to the bit and rear, or even throw itself over backward. Second, do *not* ride with the device on. It is counterproductive to do so. Third, your horse should be trained to lunge quietly in both directions and at all three gaits before the chambon is used.

Ground exercises are a valuable tool in preparing the endurance horse and are often neglected in the training program. TTEAM®, an unmounted system of training that includes body work and ground exercises to improve movement patterns, balance and focus in the horse, has a great collection of ground exercises that can help the horse in a wide variety of areas, are easy to learn and are highly effective. TTEAM is described in greater detail in Chapter 4. Pat Parelli's *Natural Horse-man-ship* program (available on video) also has some handy tools, in the form of unmounted control games and cued behaviors.

Tina Hutton, a TTEAM practitioner, works on an endurance horse's balance and engagement, using a body bandage and a neck ring.

Being ridden through the TTEAM exercise known as the maze, this horse learns to release his rib cage and bend his body through its turns. Photo: Jodi Frediani.

GYMNASTIC TRAINING IN THE ARENA

Gymnastic arena work includes riding specific, *precise* patterns at various gaits. Even if you are not a sports fan, you probably know that hulking football players are required to jog through rows of tires as a part of their training. The reason such exercises are beneficial to football players, who must dodge and weave and run, is exactly the same reason arena gymnastic patterns are useful to the endurance horse: They enable athletes to access a greater range of motion and improve their dexterity. Besides developing and expanding movement capabilities, these exercises also reduce the risk of injury.

Cavalletti are poles that lay horizontally close to the ground with premeasured spaces between them. Cavalletti are designed to increase the horse's range of motion, requiring it to lift its legs higher—which frees and works the shoulder and hip—or to lengthen or shorten its stride. The different muscle groups in the body, necessary for handling rocky trails, deep sand footing, uphill and downhill work, are all improved by work over cavalletti. The distance between cavalletti poles is adjusted according to: (1) the different gaits, (2) each horse's individual stride length, and (3) the desired effect of the work on various muscle groups. Trotting cavalletti are usually set from 4 feet, 6 inches to 5 feet apart. Cavalletti for canter work range from 9 to 12 feet

Carol Steiner from Canada enjoys schooling her horse through a cavalletti exercise at a clinic for endurance riders and their horses. Photo: Jean M. Fogle.

◄

apart. Cantering through cavalletti, when done correctly, encourages a horse to balance, round its stride and become springy, placing its front feet lightly on the ground. Poles sit about 6 to 8 inches above the ground for trotting work, and 12 to 18 inches above the ground for cantering work, and should be anchored in some type of brace to insure they do not roll. Cavalletti have been used for over a hundred years to train horses to be better movers, developing the full potential of the horse's range of motion while encouraging relaxation and tension-free movement. A level area such as an arena is recommended for cavalletti work. The flat surface eliminates the complicating factor of changing gravitational forces during the horse's early attempts to find and maintain its balance. Riding through cavalletti also helps the rider's balance.

> *When a specific motion is practiced in a repetitive manner in a calm, structured setting—for example, a gymnastic exercise designed to single out and enhance the most effective muscle groups for a given task—the brain and body of the horse relax, and efficient movement is the result.*

While I recommend the use of cavalletti as a part of a training program for endurance horses, the scope of this book neither allows for a thorough

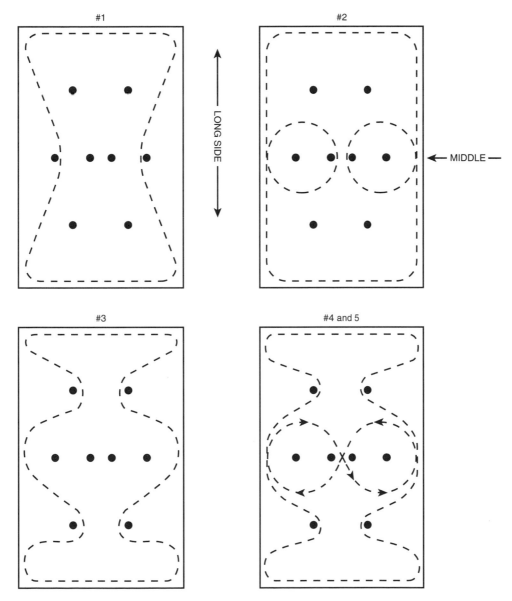

● = MARKER

This progressive series of gymnastic patterns can improve a horse's flexibility, obedience, balance, strength and mental stability.

exploration of the topic, nor can it address all the issues that should be considered before this aspect of training is undertaken. More study and/or observation of cavalletti work is both needed and recommended before you attempt more than trotting over a simple pole or two on the ground (see Appendix IV—Recommended Resources List).

Arena exercises form the cornerstone of the supple, flexible horse. The basic rules are not hard. Most riders, once they see a few diagrams and understand what the various patterns require from and develop in the horse, can compose their own course of instruction. Patterns are made up of (1) straight lines, (2) bending lines, and (3) changes of speed/gait. The rules of the game say you must try to make your horse's spine exactly match the shape of the pattern you are riding. For example, if you ride a circle 50 feet wide in a raked sand area, and stopped to look at your tracks, your horse should have kept his feet the same distance to either side of that circling line, every inch of the way around (which would be exactly what would happen if you rode him so his spine covered the line of the circle continuously the whole way around). This demand for precision is not being picky. Far from it! The repetition that is required in the muscle-firing patterns in the horse's body, as well as in balance and speed control, develops the horse gymnastically, strengthening and preparing it for the real world of the trail. The rules say: Perfect the figures and tempo, and you will reap balance, lightness, obedience and wings!

Examine the preceding diagram. It is only one example of a progressive gymnastic training pattern designed to help the horse develop suppleness, balance, strength and obedience. With this single distribution of markers (you can use road cones, buckets, cinder blocks, and so forth, and your arena can be a flat field as well as a fenced, formal riding ring), the following patterns can be ridden in a progressive training program over several weeks:

1. Kindergarten.   A long single loop on the long side of the rectangle around the single marker closest to the fence. Requires the least effort from the horse, as only a small amount of lateral flexion in its body is necessary to perform the exercise well.

2. Elementary.   A complete circle through the two center markers and back to the fence, done once on each side of the ring every time you ride around the arena. The balance required to bend the spine to this increased degree and hold the bend during the complete circle requires more muscular effort, suppleness and concentration than the Kindergarten exercise.

3. Junior High.   A double-loop pattern around the markers closest to the corners, returning to pass between the middle marker closest to the fence on the fence side; done first on one side of the arena, then on both sides of the arena several times, and finally repeated in the opposite direction. The horse must both bend and reverse the bend, and—depending on the overall length of the arena and the proximity of the cones—must organize its balance and release and contract the muscles on one side of its body or the other in rapid succession—all without losing its balance and speeding up or slowing down. All patterns are ridden in both directions during the same schooling session.

4. High School.   The double-loop pattern, same as above, with the addition of a circle (as shown) when you reach the cone at the middle of the long side. This exercise ups the ante in terms of balance, focus and muscle control.

5. College.   The same pattern as number four but there are two circles: one on the side you're currently on and one on the other side (this makes a figure eight across the width of the arena), which you ride each time you arrive at the middle cone on the long side of your area pattern.

Think this stuff is a piece of cake for a horse and rider who regularly handle mountains, woods, streams and the other aspects of the trail? Try it, but don't be surprised or frustrated if at first you find your circles are amoeba-shaped and your speedometer swings wildly up and down its mph range.

Varying your patterns is as easy as using your imagination. You can ride the figure eight alone, without riding the looping patterns before or after it, or ride any or all of the patterns shown, changing the speed within the gait or changing the gait entirely within the pattern. For example, ride the circles in walk or canter and the rest of the pattern in trot, or ride the circles in a very strong trot and the loops in a more moderate, medium tempo trot.

Every time your horse must change the bend in its body, slow down or speed up: it exercises muscle groups beyond those it would use if it were merely traveling in a straight line. A progressive pattern designed and ridden thoughtfully and repeatedly over a period of from four to six weeks, two or three times a week (think of the arena as your classroom and the time spent there as study time) will make a horse more obedient, and will increase its suppleness, balance, ability to focus and its overall muscular strength.

Endurance riders as a whole have a hard time getting their minds around the idea of working in enclosed spaces, preferring to run free mentally and physically with their horses on the trail. While I am sympathetic with that feeling, I recognize—as will the serious competitor—the benefit of progressive gymnastic body-building exercises done in an environment where it is possible to measure and compare the progress of interactive muscle groups, not just metabolics and strength. If you find yourself or your horse bored when you are in the classroom, you are not applying yourself with enough attention to your studies. When ridden correctly, a continuous forty-five-minute session of arena gymnastics can have the toughest, most experienced 100-mile competitor's tongue hanging out.

The final adventure in a gymnastic routine for the trail horse and rider, is the introduction of lateral work. Lateral work helps strengthen the abductor and adductor muscles in both the front (shoulders) and hind legs (gaskins and hindquarters). The leg yield is the simplest lateral exercise and teaches the horse to move its legs diagonally under and away from its body. It is also a great control exercise (one application is opening gates without dismounting). In order to grasp it and teach it to your horse, it is necessary to understand that the horse has six doors on his body and three buttons at slightly different places along his rib cage which, when used correctly, allow the rider to open and close the doors. The doors on a horse are the six basic directions he can send his energy once his engine is turned on.

He can go out the front door (forward), the back door (backward), toward either shoulder (you've got his nose pointed toward the trail but his feet are headed toward the trailer/barn in the direction of one shoulder or the other), or out a hip (try to back your horse in a straight line more than a few steps and you will quickly discover the hip doors that your horse has under his control). Your hands and reins provide the primary control of your horses front three doors and your seat and legs provide the primary control for the back three doors. Being able to open and close any of the doors you wish, whenever you wish, gives you control over your horse. When asked to do this exercise in clinics, many riders are surprised to discover how little control *they* really own and how much belongs to their horse. Horses don't like us to know about their doors; instead they like to surprise us by sneaking out of them to escape our control. By learning the doors and how to control them, you will find you can

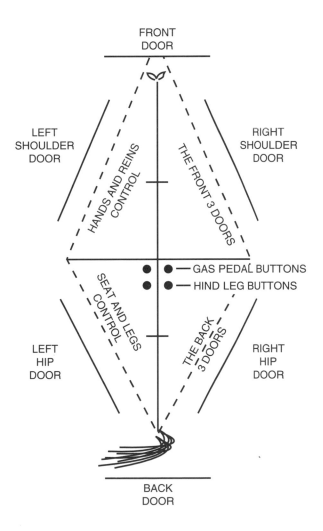

FRONT
DOOR

LEFT
SHOULDER
DOOR

HANDS AND REINS CONTROL

THE FRONT 3 DOORS

RIGHT
SHOULDER
DOOR

● ● — GAS PEDAL BUTTONS
● ● — HIND LEG BUTTONS

SEAT AND LEGS CONTROL

THE BACK 3 DOORS

LEFT
HIP
DOOR

RIGHT
HIP
DOOR

BACK
DOOR

The six doors on a horse's body and the "keys to the kingdom."

put your horse in what is known as the *corridor of the aids*. Once in this corridor, the horse has to allow you to direct its energy and eventually its mind as well. Exercises that should be practiced to help you improve your control of the different doors include the turn-on-the-forehand and turn-on-the-hindquarters. It would be best to perfect these exercises before trying the leg yield (described presently) with your horse. After you learn to control each door individually, you may use them together to send your horse's body in any direction you wish. Controlling the doors and your horse's gas pedal is, moreover, the secret to helping your horse develop a productive posture or carriage.

When riding a leg yield, aim your horse at the fence; use the hand closest to the fence to bend the horse's neck slightly, letting him look toward the fence. As your horse walks down the rail, slide your leg beside the fence a little behind the girth/cinch and press on the hind leg button (see previous diagram). You will get the best result if you alternately press and release with the horse's rhythm, rather than squeeze continuously. When your horse obeys your leg signal, it will move its hips closer to the center of the arena, so its body is at a 15° angle to the fence. It will then be moving in a crablike, sideways position down the rail. In this position, your horse must move its legs in a nonstandard way—stretching, suppling and strengthening new muscles on each side of its body. If your horse doesn't respond to your leg aids on the different buttons, teach it the correct responses by pressing on the buttons from the ground using a blunt object. Reward your horse when it moves away from the pressure with the part of its body associated with the respective button. Repeat the lesson until it has learned it fully. If your horse still doesn't seem to understand your aids when you are mounted, have a friend help by "activating" the button from the ground while you are in the saddle, reminding your horse of its groundwork training.

The shoulder-in must also be mentioned when talking about useful strengthening and suppling exercises for the trail horse. To ride the shoulder-in, the rider must wrap her horse around her inside leg, putting a bend in the horse's rib cage. This "bend" causes the horse to experience isometric resistance from its own body when moving through the various exercises it is performing, while maintaining a shoulder-fore or shoulder-in position. I do not believe this exercise can be taught in the pages of a book. Seek an instructor that uses dressage as a training tool and is experienced with the demands of endurance riding to help you and your horse advance to this step.

Consider taking some lessons during the winter months when your access to the trail is restricted by adverse weather. With a good teacher, you and your horse will become better, stronger competitors. Many international riders work with a coach on a regular basis to enhance and improve their performance.

GYMNASTIC TRAINING ON THE TRAIL

Gymnastic training is not limited to the arena: it is only begun there. Once you have laid the foundation for your horse to understand and obey your various aids for controlling direction of movement, power, and length of stride, gymnastic work can be incorporated as a part of time spent on the trail. On a wide dirt road, ride a circle or two the width of the road, then move on. Ride zigzag patterns around a line of trees in a field or through a row of bushes. After you become used to thinking in gymnastic figures you will see them everywhere along the trail. You only have to pick one out and ride it to school your horse while you condition it.

When you find a wide trail, you can do some leg yields—moving the horse with your leg aids from one side of the road to the other and back again in diagonal lines. On narrow confining trails, work on longitudinal suppling by lengthening and shortening the horse's frame and stride at all gaits. The more supple the horse becomes, the less energy it uses to move over the ground. Gymnastic work on the trail continues the strengthening and balancing process for your horse by

- Making all its muscle groups more flexible, resilient, and resistant to fatigue or accidents.

- Increasing the horse's confidence by expanding its athletic abilities.

- Building your horse's trust in you through the constant conversation of the aids.

You are the one who knows how far your horse must go today, how hard he must work in what section of the trail, when he should conserve his energy and when he should spend it. For you to do your best as a team, however, your horse must be a full and willing partner in your decisions on ride day

HILL WORK

There is a common fallacy among endurance riders about horses and hills. It is that a horse is either an "uphill" horse (meaning he can go uphill exceptionally well) or he is a "downhill" horse (meaning he can go downhill very fast). The truth is, if a horse is biomechanically designed to do either of these activities well, it can be trained and strengthened to do the other equally as well.

Think of hill work as weightlifting for your horse. If done correctly, with the horse in a good correct frame, slow work up hills (first walking, then at a slow trot) is the fastest way to strengthen a horse's hindquarters. All hill work should be *gradually* increased, starting with gentle slopes, both up and down, increasing the degree of climb or descent as the horse increases its strength and stamina. Overworking a young horse is easy to do when riding mountainous terrain. Hill work done wrong is a direct route to injury.

With the muscles of his neck and back contracted and tight, this horse's hocks are taking a severely increased stress load as the horse tries to move its mass up the hill in opposition to its rider's position and its own tension.

This horse is displaying an efficient posture while ascending a hill.

When hill work is first begun (at walk), increase the rear leg loading one side at a time and for short periods by bending the horse's neck slightly and causing it to put its nose in front of one shoulder or the other as it pushes itself up the incline. This is isometric exercise. Watch your horse for muscular changes in the rear end. With regular graduated work, you will be able to see his body change and develop in about three months. His hindquarters will look rounder (not hollow as so many endurance horses look), his interior gaskin muscles will develop, making his gaskin appear to be wider when viewed from behind. If his poll is at the same height (or lower) as his withers as he climbs, the muscles of his neck just in front of his shoulder will fill out, giving his top line a more "rounded" appearance.

Downhill work is started in walk with halts every 100 feet or so. As the horse gets stronger, add one complete step of backup (each hind leg must move back one step) every time you halt. Make sure the hill on which you begin training is only a gentle slope, especially when you add the backup exercise to your training. When you ask your horse to back up a hill, before you apply any pressure on the bit to signal the backward step, lighten your seat in the saddle and ask your horse to get under itself with its hind legs first. If the horse is unwilling to back up and you apply excessive pressure on his mouth to force him to do so, he will raise his head out of position, drop his back and can damage his hocks when backing.

You will gradually notice your horse start to carry its front end, stepping lightly with its front feet, as it makes its way downhill. At the same time you will also notice the horse is putting its hind legs more deeply under its body with each stride. When you notice these changes, you can begin to train the downhill in a trot. Start slow at first, building the holding muscles of the hindquarters, just like you built the pushing muscles with the uphill work. Intersperse the trot periods with walk periods, especially if it is a long down-hill trail. During this phase of training, your horse will progress more rapidly if you are a good enough rider to offer steady, nonabusive contact with the bit. This light contact makes the horse feel supported and allows it to respond more freely when first asked to increase its downhill speed at trot.

The ultimate downhill trot happens when the horse fires, or turns on, his holding muscles *only when his feet are on the ground*. This means the horse's muscles are relaxed during each suspension phase of the trot (there are two suspension phases to each full stride of trot). The horse saves energy by allow-ing gravity to move him down the hill for the short span of time between diagonal strides. Unhindered by an unbalanced or tight rider, a horse who moves in this manner downhill can fly down the steepest terrain without putting a foot wrong and with almost no muscular effort to speak of. He is the classic downhill horse that endurance riders talk about. What you need to remember is—*any horse* can be taught to do this, given enough time, good riding, and the correct technique.

TAILING

Tailing is used by endurance riders as a way of climbing hills while saving the horse's energy. It involves following behind your horse, holding on to its tail and letting the horse pull you up the hill behind it. To begin training your horse to tail, start by simply working carefully around your horse's hind end: grooming, brushing the tail, etc., until you can handle the horse's tail without any signs of resistance from the horse (such as clamping the tail to the buttocks when the tail is handled). Then stand behind the horse, wrap the end of its tail around your hand, and slowly lean your weight against it. Never forget you are in a dangerous position when you work around a horse's hind feet. Stay alert for signs of fright in the horse, and be ready to step to one side or the other if the horse shows signs of nervousness because you are behind him. If your horse accepts you pulling on his tail with no problem, have a friend lead the horse around a familiar place while you walk behind and just off to one side of him, holding onto his tail. When he accepts this without question, apply pressure by pulling on the tail as your horse is led around. Finally, find a small hill and have a friend lead your horse up the hill while you hold onto its tail, letting it pull you up the hill after it.

When your horse accepts all of the above, snap some thin cotton lines to the bit and drive the horse around, staying just to one side or the other where the horse can see you and the line out of the corner of its eye. Be careful when first letting the outside line touch your horse in the area of its buttocks or hocks, as some horses may startle from this and attempt to rush forward, or turn and look at what is touching them. If you think your horse might do this, get a handler for the front end until your horse accepts the feel of the lines on its body. You can run your lines through the stirrups to keep them from getting tangled in your horse's legs. Finally, take one line in the hand you have wrapped in the tail and the other line in your free hand and drive your horse while you tail it. Most endurance horses catch on quickly and can soon be tailed with only one line instead of two.

CONDITIONING AND FEEDING

Your conditioning regimen, whether for you or your horse, is going to depend on five basic factors: (1) age, (2) present state of health/fitness, (3) fitness/health history, (4) level of competition for which you are preparing, and (5) experience in the field.

CONDITIONING THE RIDER

If you are 55, have been riding for a short three months, have spent most of your adult life in a chair behind a desk, and want to do Tevis (100 miles in one day over the Sierra Nevada mountains), it will take a while for you to prepare; perhaps a year or two. If you are 25, run, bike, or hike 20 miles or more a week, work out for an hour every day, have been riding since you were ten (even if it was in the show arena) and want to try a local 50-mile ride in the rolling hills of Georgia; with a fit horse, some instruction and three or four weeks of preparation, you'll do just fine.

Most riders I know ride to stay fit. If you ride enough to condition your own horse for a 50-mile ride, you will most likely be able to handle a 50-mile ride, especially if you pick an easy ride (lots of flat ground) for your first experience. The same goes for your first 100-mile ride. When you decide to set your cap to win, place in the top ten or get regional or national awards, your personal conditioning regimen can become more diverse and aggressive. If, however, you start out unfit, and/or overweight, riding as your sole source of exercise will not bring you to the necessary state of fitness.

Nonriding activities like walking and swimming help to prepare you for long periods in the saddle and increase your overall fitness. I recommend walking over running. Running shortens your Achilles tendons (in riding, your Achilles tendons need to be long and flexible to allow for proper shock absorption through the ankle joints), and thickens the quadricep muscles. There is also more chance of impact-related stress injuries with running. If you are over thirty and have never run, starting requires a conservative approach and should include a physical with advice from your doctor as well as a sports coach. Walking can be done at any age.

Swimming is a great way to increase your flexibility and stamina. The drawback is finding an all-weather place to swim. Walking is available to you any time, especially when you are on the trail. Walk your horse as a part of your training routine. Walk until you are tired, then ride again. As you gain more fitness, walk up hills, resting when you need to. There is no one in charge of your time table except you. Walking downhill requires a different set of muscles. While it may seem easier and requires less energy, if you overdo the downhill distances in the beginning, you will be sore, so limit your downhill walking, increasing the distance and degree of slope gradually. The same is true for your uphill work. Listen to your heart rate and breathing patterns and stop to rest before you become exhausted. Gaining a few feet every day in comfort is the way to accelerate to the top in the fitness game. Rabbits aren't stayers and a stayer is what is needed in the sport of endurance riding.

It is always a good idea to stretch before you ride and if you are a rider who jogs or runs to stay fit, stretching is vitally important to offset the undesirable, muscle-shortening effects of running. Stretches that benefit a rider include calf, hamstring, quadricep and groin stretches, and low, middle and upper back and side stretches. A great book on stretching featuring clearly drawn, simple to understand, effective stretches, is Bob Anderson's *Stretching*. Regular use of what you find there will enhance your ability as a rider and competitor.

In order to be physically healthy you must eat well. A diet of high fat and sugar will not support the physical effort you will need during a ride. Balance (riding, walking and/or swimming) and patience (don't expect to accomplish every change you want in 30 days or less) in both eating and exercising is the best way to arrive at a sound state of health and fitness.

Mental discipline and fitness is as much a part of the sport as physical fitness. Emotions can wreck an effort as fast as low blood sugar. If you get upset because the rider in front of you won't let you pass on a narrow trail, you can watch your energy level drop. Some level of depression is a pitstop on every 100-mile ride. If you are unaware of what is happening and let yourself stay in this state, it may cost you the ride. Horses know if you are depressed, tense or angry. What they won't know is why. If you allow yourself to get trapped in a negative emotional state for very long, it will tire both you and your horse. If you find this happening find another rider to buddy-up with on the trail. Talk, tell stories, sing, be silly, anything to change your mental state. Your horse will also respond in a positive way to the company of another horse and you can let your horses take turns leading. The horse in front will act like the engine of a train, and pull along the horse behind it.

Get used to the fact that you may be spending time alone during a ride. If this is your idea of heaven, you have no problem, but if strange noises in the woods at night tend to send you into a panic, consider the steps you must take to insure you don't add that burden to the physical challenges the trail provides. The trail will find and test all your weaknesses, especially at the 100-mile distance. Your mental ride plan for you and your horse needs to take into account your personality type. It won't benefit you to substitute frustration at having to slow down in order to have company for fear of being alone. Even if you have planned for a riding partner going into the ride, nothing says he or she won't be pulled before the finish. Thinking through such possibilities will prepare you to handle them if they should happen during an event.

When riding in extreme weather conditions, pay attention to the needs of your body as well as those of your horse. You wouldn't be the first rider to have had to pull yourself from a ride because you became dehydrated, overheated, or hypothermic. Besides feeling bad physically, you end up feeling bad emotionally for letting your horse down as well!

Work your way up in small steps to whatever goals you dream about. You can choose to see undesirable events along the way as either roadblocks or challenges. Successful riders see problems as challenges. Fears, such as of heights, of being alone, of snakes, of failure, even fear of success, need to be recognized and accepted as challenges that have to be addressed before they reduce the effectiveness of your performance on the trail.

CONDITIONING THE HORSE

No book can give you a realistic day-by-day training schedule that will work all the time, because you and your horse are individuals with a thousand different circumstances that impact a conditioning schedule. If you are not able or willing to listen to your horse and learn from him, your success as an endurance rider will be limited. Having warned you that (1) your knowledge of your horse, (2) your ability to observe, register what you observed and respond to it appropriately, (3) your common sense, and (4) your gut feelings are your greatest allies in this game, I will give you some conditioning guidelines that have worked for me over the years.

In the sixties, the initials LSD stood for a mind-altering drug. In endurance LSD stands for Long Slow Distance training and it is still a mind-altering drug, but in a different way. It is also the road to success in the world of endurance riding. Although experienced riders talk about doing LSD training, as you spend time around the endurance scene it quickly becomes evident that one rider's LSD is another's sprint. So what is LSD and how long should training at the LSD level take? Long slow distance riding is just that. Long can be 10 miles in the first month of a four-year-old horse's conditioning schedule or it can be 35 miles of trailing behind a herd of cattle from sunup to sundown for a horse whose fitness is several years into its development. David, an extremely wise cowboy, once told me his secret for starting his horses (he would put them under saddle at three, a practice I don't recommend because too few people can do it without causing long-term damage to their horse's physical structure). What he said was "Never turn the hair on their neck." What he meant was that during the LSD phase of training, which could last up to two years with three to four months off during the winter (this translates to between 12 and 18 months of riding), he never rode his colts hard enough to heat them up enough to cause them to sweat. He could ride young 'uns all day long, making them stronger and stouter until, by the winter of their second season with him, what started as a spindly legged, narrow-chested, wobbly baby was transformed into a muscular, powerful, savvy, four-wheel-drive machine, which could go anywhere with ease, incredible staying power, and unending energy. *The Man From Snowy River* had nothing on my friend when it came to where he could and would go with his horses! Over the years I watched him do this with colt after colt. They all stayed sound, and by the time they were six year olds, they covered 30 to 40 miles a day, week in and week out, and at the end of the day looked as if they had never left the ranch. When he shared his reasoning behind his approach to conditioning a horse with me, I listened.

> I think nature is your best friend when you're trying to condition a horse. If I can take them to the edge of what nature gave them for that day, but never cross that line, at night when I put them up, nature replaces what I've used. To protect that horse, she gives it one more mile than what that horse needed today. Tomorrow, when I ride that colt again, I can go 7/8ths of a mile further before I reach the line I never want to cross. That way nature and I work together to make my horses strong.

What David with his cowboy-savvy observations and experience had discovered is the same thing that scientists doing studies on the cannon bones of young race horses have discovered. If the horse is used without being overused, it gets stronger. The trick is to find a way of knowing where the line is between use and overuse before you cross it. For my friend, the horse's internal temperature was his barometer.

Your LSD program should be a two-year program, since it takes two years to strengthen bones sufficiently. Shortcuts in this phase of training threaten the *long*-term soundness of a horse. It takes a less amount of time—between 12 and 18 months—to strengthen ligaments and tendons. This timetable is based on the assumption you don't override the horse and need to factor in recovery time. Most riders know they must take their time developing a young horse, but may get into a hurry when conditioning a mature horse. Conditioning *from scratch* takes approximately the same amount of time whether the horse is four or fourteen. Muscles condition the quickest, in about six months. An overweight pleasure horse who has never been out of a stall and/or paddock in its entire life, except to be worked for an hour in an arena three times a week, will need more time in the LSD phase just to get rid of fat around its internal organs, than a horse the same age who has spent its idle hours exercising itself on a side hill with only moderate amounts of food.

Just like with the rider, walking is the place to start. Most of your first-year LSD training will be done at the walk and slow trot. In the second year of conditioning, you will still spend up to 30 percent or more of your time in walk, but now the walk will increase in speed and become purposeful—a power walk that is going somewhere—and you will ask your horse to hold that power walk up hills as well as on the flat, to help develop the driving muscles of the hind end.

You will also increase your trot in speed and duration. When introducing short-distance-conditioning days with more speed, your ride will range between 10 and 15 miles, consist of 65 percent second-gear (10 mph) trot, and will begin to include some steeper hill work (returning to walk when you first increase the degree of incline in hill work). After several months of work in second-gear trot, you will include several periods of 1 to 2 miles in third gear (14–15 mph) trot. Somewhere between the end of the second year and the beginning of the third conditioning year, I begin serious speed work: third-gear trot for periods of up to 10 miles at a time and canters and gallops working up to 5 miles or more. I also include short sprints (1/2 mile) uphills at full gallop to work the heart and lungs, followed by a "first gear" (7-mph trot) until the horse is recovered. When speed work is begun you can introduce interval training, using two rides of 5 miles on the same day, separated by a one- to two-hour rest period. A LSD ride should be included about once a week until your horse is in his third year, when competitions can replace some of your conditioning miles. If you are running up front by the third year of competition or before, you should not be racing your horse more than once a month and your other work should include LSD rides as well as your galloping workouts and your heart and lung sprint/hill work.

Downhill work at trot is hard on the horse until he learns to carry his weight with the muscles of his hind end. It should be postponed to the second year of conditioning, when his balance training and flat work will have better prepared him to do the work without damaging himself.

A conditioning program consists of slow changes. Each change in routine should increase the demand on your horse just a little bit. For instance, you should never increase the distance *and* the speed at the same time. Another way of increasing the work load for the horse is to change the footing (20 minutes of deep sand work at trot is equal to an hour of trot work on normal footing) or topography (steep hill work requires more from the horse than rolling hills or flat land).

Factors which increase stress are: distance, weight carried, speed, terrain (flat versus hills), footing (sand versus rocks versus grass), and temperature. A good conditioning program must factor in *all* of those items *and* be able to adjust for them in the overall length of the session. That is why no one can write an exact training program for you and your horse without knowing your precise circumstances. Your ability to assess your horse's present state of fitness and then design a conditioning program to maintain and/or improve it will be one of the major hurdles you master to become a successful endurance rider—no matter whether you just want to finish or be among the top ten.

Common Sense

- No book can take the place of your horse to tell you how much, how fast and for how long you should go on any given training day or any given ride.

- It takes two years of LSD to build a base from which to compete.

- If you live in a climate that doesn't let you ride your horse year-round, factor that into your thinking when figuring up the number of years you have spent conditioning your horse.

- Commonsense is the single ingredient that, when missing, causes the greatest damage to horses.

If you are lucky enough to have access to a place where you can swim your horse I recommend this exercise be included in your conditioning program. It is also an excellent way to rehab a horse during or following an injury. Swimming works both the heart and lungs and is a good way to stretch out contracted muscles after an injury, returning them to suppleness without risk of overuse and reinjury. Swimming is frequently used by the racing industry in its training programs, so if you want or need to swim your horse, start there to find information on locations to swim your horse.

Most books use the number of miles ridden in their conditioning formulas; but it is my experience that few trails are measured. If you are riding on Park Service land, National Forest, etc. and stay to marked trails, there may be maps that you can use to figure out the approximate mileage of your conditioning rides. A better way to get a handle on the distance of any given conditioning ride is to know the rate of speed (in mph) your horse is traveling. To be sure of your training distances, find a section of trail you can measure accurately (with an odometer on a dirt bike?) and ride your horse on it regularly at different gaits. Note your time for each gait and your speed within a gait, until you can set your horse at a desired miles per hour pace and keep him there by feel. It's not hard to do, but does take practice besides the initial work of measuring and marking a specific distance. If it takes 30 minutes for your horse to walk one mile, he is traveling at 2 mph. If you go the mile in 15 minutes, his speed is 4 mph. Thus, 12 minutes equals 5 mph, 10 equals 6 mph, 7 1/2 equals 8 mph, and so forth.

Keeping track of the time it takes you to ride that one mile at each gait will give you a base from which to figure your overall mileage on a training ride. You will also learn pace control, a valuable asset in competition. A county fairground with a race track is a good place for this phase of your training. To decide if you want to pursue this precise approach to conditioning, ask yourself how serious a competitor you want to become. If you are finishing rides now and want to move up, you are going to have to go the extra mile, no pun intended. World-class champions dedicate a lot of time and thought to their sport. Their success is not accidental. On the other hand, getting across the finish line with a sound horse each time you start a ride is a win of another kind and does not require the same effort as staying at the top.

All performance horses are subject to injury and endurance horses are no exception. The following list includes some common injuries that could happen to your horse and the length of time they could affect your conditioning schedule:

- Tying up (lactic acidosis):   A couple of days to a week or more

- Saddle or girth sores: One week to a month

- Tears in muscle, tendons or ligaments: Six weeks to 6 months or more

- Joint injuries (inflammation):   Eight weeks to a year

- Hoof injuries (bruises, corns, cracks):   Two weeks to 6 months

- Bone damage (arthritic changes):   Irreversible

If your horse should injure himself during conditioning or competition, you can help by doing the following:

- Noticing and diagnosing the problem early.

- Designing a plan (with the help of your vet if necessary) to rehabilitate him, including modifying your competition schedule if necessary.

- Implementing the plan and watching the horse for input (written notes are a good way of keeping track of daily changes).

- Preventing reinjury.

When considering the subject of conditioning it is necessary to speak about the mental conditioning of the long-distance horse. Horses are creatures of habit. If you want to do 100-mile rides with your horse, it is best to enter an easy 100 as soon as your horse is in good enough condition to complete that distance without injury. This should not happen before his second year of competition, or before he is six years old. If you delay exposing him to the longer distance, he will become mentally conditioned to being finished at 50 miles. While his physical conditioning may enable him to do the greater distance, when he is asked to go out on the trail again after 50 or 60 miles, his mental state could sabotage his physical efforts and/or his recoveries.

Many if not most endurance horses are kept in pastures or at least large paddocks and, when possible, these two options provide the very best of environments. Sometimes, however, it is simply not possible to avoid stalling a horse, especially if confinement is necessary in the event of an injury. The smart rider thinks about such a situation and conditions her horse to accept the confinement of a stall by exposing him to the situation in increasing degrees. Start by confining him during the day and letting him out at night; then keep him in for two days and turn him out for 24 hours. Finally, stall him and turn him out to play for a an hour each day, until he learns to accept, without agitation or resentment, a confined situation. If you fail to address this aspect of your horse's mental conditioning, you run the risk of penalizing your horse at a time when he needs his energy and focus to do his best in an event. The same holds true with trailering and standing tied. If the horse objects to either of these things, he will not travel well, and will put himself at risk of injury or arriving at an event in poor condition. If he frets all night long because he must stand tied to the side of the trailer or be enclosed in a stall, he will be less fit for the next day's competition.

Horses, being herd animals, are quick to form bonds. An attachment to another horse can create an enormous problem if that horse is unable to start or continue a ride and your horse has to go out alone. If the situation is reversed, your horse may become violent when his buddy is taken away, tearing up his portable corral, struggling against his halter if tied or breaking out completely, endangering himself and others. A herd-bound horse can waste excessive amounts of energy trying to stay up with horses in front of him, or become so aggressive in his desire to be out front that he hurts himself or his rider. Any excessive behavior of this type puts your horse at risk physically, and saps his strength and stamina during a ride. It is also accompanied by an unstable mental state that puts the rider at risk as well.

Most of these behaviors can be minimized, if not entirely eliminated, if you take the time to condition your horse to the circumstances before experiencing them at a ride. Take for example the horse who either needs to be in front or only wants to follow. As a part of mental conditioning for their horses, I have my clients practice the merry-go-round game. A number of riders, from as few as three or four to as many as eight, go for a ride together. When they hit a two-wide trail they form a single file on the right edge of the road. Start the game at walk. The last horse in line pulls to the left, and is asked for a brisk walk and allowed to pass all the other horses, going to the front of the line, where his rider returns him to the right side of the road and takes the lead for a short time. The riders being passed work to slow their horses while maintaining the same gait. The game continues until every horse has been to the front at least once. If the width of the trail permits, you can continue the game for as long as you like, rotating through all the gaits, including canter.

While playing the game, after a few rotations, I will move the line over to the left side of the road so the horses learn to pass each other and accept being passed on either side. After a few rotations, horses learn their turn will come to be in front and this helps them to be patient and wait their turn. Little by little, the timid horse (follower) finds his courage because he knows he only has to stay out front for a short time before he is rescued from his fear by another horse passing him. The game also offers riders the chance to work on rating their horses, allowing them to perfect the control necessary for both their safety and their horse's safety in the group situations inherent in the sport. A horse offering to kick or crowd another horse should be disciplined quickly. Some riders like the aggressive attitude their horses display towards horses who attempt to pass, feeling it gives them an edge in controlling the trail. While a timid horse might hesitate to pass an aggressive one if the aggressive horse is displaying threatening body language, it only takes a second for a kick to shatter bones and cause permanent injury or death. Riding will always have some risk, but preventable injury has no place in the sport and most certainly should not be there to insure someone has a greater chance of getting over the finish line first. You are responsible for your horse's manners, and tying a red ribbon in his tail is not a substitute for discipline and training.

TTEAM®

In my forty-plus years with horses, the Linda Tellington-Jones Equine Awareness Method work (TTEAM for short) is one of the best systems of education and body work for helping the equine athlete perform and recover that it has been my pleasure to encounter. The system is relatively easy to learn and its benefits are endless. There are videotapes and seminars throughout the country that teach TTEAM techniques to owners and riders. I recommend it strongly to riders who care about their horses, want an edge in competition by giving their horses every recovery advantage possible, or need to change negative or dangerous behavior in their horses. Linda Tellington-Jones (founder of TTEAM) and practitioners trained by her are often engaged to work on horses at major international events in several disciplines, including endurance. More information about these advanced, humane, simple-to-do techniques for reducing stress and increasing a horse's ability to learn is available by contacting the TTEAM office at 800-854-8326 or writing to them at P.O. Box 3793, Santa Fe, New Mexico, 87501.

Training With The Heart Monitor

Today's rider has the advantage of modern technology in the form of the heart monitor. While I strongly believe you should learn to read your horse, not just your electronics, it would be foolish not to take advantage of this piece of equipment in order to insure your conditioning program is on target and to help learn the pace at which your horse can maintain his optimum performance for the longest amount of time. Another important use of the heart monitor is as an early warning device. If your horse is experiencing pain or discomfort somewhere in his body—or is ill—his heart rate will tell you by being higher than normal, or refusing to drop as quickly as it normally would. If you use a heart monitor, do not wear it on the same wrist as a digital watch, because a digital watch can interfere with the reception of some monitors.

There are two types of exercise: (1) aerobic, where the horse's heart is able to provide enough oxygen to the body to keep up with the physiological demands of performance, and (2) anaerobic, or work without the benefit of oxygen. A horse held in anaerobic work for very long becomes fatigued more quickly than one in aerobic work, because waste products like lactic acid accumulate in the muscle cells. When your horse's heart rate rises over 150 beats per minute, he is beginning to do anaerobic work. Below that he is working aerobically. While it is necessary to push your horse into anaerobic work periodically during conditioning in order to strengthen the heart muscle and teach his body how to become efficient at transporting and using oxygen, if your horse's heart rate goes over 200 bpm, most of the work is anaerobic work. The longer the heart must work anaerobically, the slower it will recover when it has the opportunity to rest. If one minute after pulling up, your horse's heart rate is still above 130 bpm, your horse was working at a rate that if prolonged could produce injury. If, on the other hand, his heart rate is less than 100 bpm one minute after you've stopped, your work isn't doing much to improve his cardiovascular system. Building a strong heart and cardiovascular system in the endurance horse takes time. Your horse must be brought to a stage of fitness where he can maintain a heart rate of at least 150 to 200 bpm for periods of a half hour at a time without becoming unduly fatigued by the effort (by the third year of conditioning). Cardiovascular work should *not* be done every day as your horse needs recovery time between workouts. Two to three times a week is sufficient in the second year of training.

The on-board heart monitor also gives you an advantage at vet checks since the vets can easily watch the heart rate and make necessary vetting decisions based on what the horse's heart rate is telling them. To really take advantage of the heart monitor during training, you need to keep a log book and record your horse's heart rates during various types of training over the same trail. Since heat will impact a horse's recovery, it is also necessary to pay attention to temperature during your training periods to let the heart rate be an accurate guide to stress. A horse may start out with a higher rate at the beginning of the season, but as it becomes better conditioned, the same work over the same trail for the same amount of time will produce a lower heart rate. This is how you know your horse's condition is improving. Another interesting fact that can be determined by use of the heart monitor is whether your horse is a galloping horse or a trotting horse. Contrary to popular belief, some horses use more energy at trot than at canter. If your horse happens to be one of them, you will want to know it and use the canter whenever possible during a ride to allow your horse to function at his maximum efficiency level.

The AERC medication policy's list of permissible substances (preceding and during competition) includes

- Vitamins

- Minerals

- Electrolytes

- Liniments that do not contain materials absorbed into the body (alcohol and Absorbine)

- Foodstuffs known as nutrients

- Nonabsorbable topical wound dressings

- Alcohol

- Ice and ice water

- Compounds to synchronize estrus.

Nonpermissible substances include

- Any substance by injection or stomach tube

- Vitamins in megadoses

- Nutrient substances administered in doses to achieve a pharmacologic effect (DMSO, DMG, yucca and MSM)

- Any anti-inflammatory, stimulants, depressants, analgesia or analgesia-containing products such as procaine penicillin

- Antihistaminic

- Vasoactive

- Bronchodilator

- Masking substances (sulfa drugs, benzimadole wormers, thiamine injections)

- Dipyrone

- Lazix

- Trimethoprim

- Liniments that contain DMSO, menthol or camphor

- E-SE injections

Alternative Support Therapies

Riders today have an array of alternative support therapies upon which to draw to keep their horses at the peak of their game and/or help rehabilitate them if they become injured. Like forbidden drugs, alternative support therapies such as chiropractic, acupuncture, cold laser, magnets and ultrasound can not be administered during the period of the ride, but massage and stretching are permitted.

Adequan   An injectable substance developed for use in horses that are subjected to performance stress. It is used primarily for the purposes of pain relief in acute and chronic degenerative joint disease. Endurance riders and at least one vet I know use it as a preventative, since it improves the lubricating properties of the horse's natural joint fluid. You might say it helps put a Teflon surface around the end of the bones where they meet at joints.

Massage   A physical manipulation of the muscles, tendons and ligaments of the horse in a series of rubbing patterns to stimulate blood flow, relaxation and tension release. I use basic massage when I work on my horses during a ride. I also get massaged personally and know its benefits by its effects on my body. Massage has proven to be a great tool in keeping top athletes, both human and equine performing at the peak of their game.

Acupuncture   Needles, heat or electricity are used in this therapy to stimulate specific nerve fibers to clear and balance energy-flow patterns within the body. Many more vets today are exploring the healing properties of acupuncture. I have used acupuncture to advantage as a part of my routine care for horses whose symptoms would not respond to other approaches. Acupressure is a form of acupuncture that utilizes pressure to stimulate specific "trigger" points on the body.

Cold Laser   This treatment stimulates tissue at a cellular level, helping to produce rapid healing and pain relief. BioScan is an example of a cold laser system. It is designed for use by the layman and has produced remarkable changes in a number of horses. I use and recommend the tendon boots ($200.00) for tendon and ligament problems, as well as the light patch ($100.00) for back sensitivity and open wound care. An entire diagnostic and treatment system costs around $5,000.00.

Ultrasound   This procedure is used to identify injury in the musculoskeletal structures. It can also be used to treat injuries because of its ability to create heat in deep tissue. With today's technological advances, it is no longer necessary to guess whether your horse has done serious damage to its tendons and ligaments. Your vet can diagnose a multiple of problems with an ultrasound "x-ray." Being certain about such conditions can prevent further injury through early treatment or reduce lay-up time.

Stretching   This exercise is a form of tension release and can produce more flexible muscles, which in turn are better able to perform well under stress. An excellent video on stretching is *Basic Equine Stretching* by Nancy Spencer. I teach all my athletes to do basic stretches and use them in my daily training and conditioning routines.

Chiropractic   A feature of this therapy is the manipulation and realigning of the bones of the spine and body. It is the form of therapy that has produced the greatest and most immediate effects on my horses. Exploring its uses with a qualified practitioner is an avenue I recommend for top competitors and concerned owners.

Herbal Remedies   Herbs have long been used to help relieve or cure conditions in people and animals. Herbals also offer some alternative therapy possibilities that have shown interesting results. Arnica Montana is an herbal remedy I use in my barn for the treatment of inflammation. Bach's Rescue Remedy is another all-purpose herbal I keep on hand and use regularly when the need arises.

Magnets   It has been said that magnets help to heal by increasing the blood flow to specific areas of the body. They have been used in human athletes to speed recovery from intense training and are available in blankets and leg wraps for use on horses.

Shoeing

A good farrier is your horse's best ally. The age-old adage "No foot, no horse" is as true today as it was hundreds of years ago. The endurance rider who doesn't shoe his or her own horses will need to find a knowledgeable farrier— one who will listen, so you can act as a team to see your horse has what it needs in the important area of shoeing. Pay whatever it costs to get the best work possible and have a good backup farrier as well. If your horse throws a shoe three days before a ride and your farrier is stuck on jury duty, you can call your backup farrier and still get your horse's shoe replaced in time. Plan your horse's shoeing schedule at the beginning of the year when you plan your ride schedule. Learn to read the wear marks on your horse's shoes during your training and competitive season to make sure your horse is landing on and breaking over his foot in a balanced manner. A change in wear marks during a season can also be an early warning sign and should not be ignored. Your farrier can instruct you in how to read a shoe and if he or she can't, start looking for a new farrier.

How to Keep your Farrier Happy.

- Provide a dry, sheltered, flat, shady, fly-free area for him or her to work in.

- Make appointments in advance and be on time.

- Teach your horse manners, so he is easy to shoe and will stand quietly without trying to jerk his feet away or lean his weight on the leg that is being held up.

- Pay your bills immediately and cheerfully.

- If you question something about the way your farrier shod your horse, ask him. Don't ask everyone else at your barn and then tell him what they said.

- Bake cookies for him and remember to say thank you.

Shoeing charges vary, running from a low of about $45.00 for a set of ordinary shoes to a high of $125.00 with special shoes, or when extra fitting work is required. No matter what the price, if the job is done well every time and your farrier helps you monitor changes in your horse's movement patterns by calling your attention to unusual wear on its shoes, it is worth every penny.

There are almost as many different types of shoes for horses as there are for people. Some useful nonstandard shoes include lightweight, wide-web shoes, aluminum eggbars, wedge shoes (to provide elevation for low heels) and rim shoes. Some riders prefer not to shoe their horses, keeping them barefoot, and using Easy Boots for competition. Keep in mind, shoe weight alters a horse's stride. I like to keep my horses in the lightest shoes possible that offer the degree of support and protection to the foot that is necessary. A heavy shoe causes the horse to use more shoulder muscle to move the leg, lifting rather than swinging it (a waste of energy in a horse whose primary job is to cover distance). If your horse loses a shoe during a ride, it would be courting disaster for the replacement shoe to be significantly heavier than the shoes on its other feet.

If your horse suffers from thin walls or cracking, have your farrier use thin, long nails, (they use them in shoeing gaited horses) breaking them out high on the hoof wall. Then use a feed supplement like Biotin to encourage strong hoof growth in your horse. The regular application of a good hoof dressing, such as Rain Maker, is recommended. It will help prevent the hoof from absorbing too much moisture too fast when the weather turns wet, or from losing valuable moisture in a hotter climate/time of year. Changes in the moisture content of the hoof are directly related to loss of shoes and indirectly related to soundness issues.

Learning to recognize balance in a horse's foot is something that takes some time and study. Ask your farrier questions to help improve your eye whenever possible. Read articles (such as the "Balanced Foot" articles by endurance vet Dr. Nancy Loving in *Trail Blazer Magazine*) whenever you can find them, and make time to attend at least one or two seminars or classes on shoeing.

Should your horse come up lame a day or two after a shoeing, a *close nail* (a nail that is putting pressure on the sensitive laminae of the foot) may be the problem. An easy way to check this is to take a small hammer and tap the wall of the hoof on top of the clinch for each nail. If the problem is a close nail, most horses will react when that nail is struck with the hammer. The more you know about your horse's feet, the art of shoeing and what is available in the way of foot wear for your horse, the better you will be able to evaluate his shoeing and make decisions about the type of shoes you want for the type of ride the horse is facing.

Nutrition Notes

- 2 cups canola or corn oil = 1 pound = 4000 calories

- 1 pound alfalfa = 1000 calories (high in calcium)

- 1 pound sudan hay = 800 calories (high in calcium)

- Rice bran is high in fat and phosphorus

- Horses need a ratio of 1.2 parts calcium to 1 part phosphorus in their diets.

- Alfalfa hay has a higher protein content than oat hay.

- Good grass or timothy hay is the best hay for horses.

Feeding

Before addressing the subject of what feed stuffs to offer your horse, let me point out that without a regular and thorough worming program and a regular (once a year) visit by an equine dentist, your horse will not be able to fully utilize its food.

Paste wormers are readily available, with ivermectin being the wormer that provides the greatest kill rate of the largest variety of worms. Horses should be wormed once every 8 to 10 weeks.

While veterinarians regularly "float" (file) a horse's teeth to keep down sharp edges, they are not equine dentists. When doctors first started practicing medicine on humans, they would pull a bad tooth. Today, no doctor would think of trying to do the specialized work of the dental field. It is the same with horses. Many horses have tooth, bite, and alignment problems that far exceed the training scope of most veterinarians. Having your horse checked once a year by someone who has been trained to recognize and correct these problems is an important part of your equine athlete's maintenance program.

"What's the best thing to feed a horse?" is one of the most controversial questions in the horse world. Ask one hundred riders/owners and you will get one hundred different answers—so let's start with some basics before we venture into specifics. Whatever hay you use, it should be the best you can buy, weed free, as well as free of dust and (especially) mold. Feeding dusty or moldy hay can cause damage to a horse's lungs, reducing your horse's ability to

Some horses need to be taught to drink when water is offered to them. Photo: Genie Stewart-Spears. ➤

perform by damaging his ability to breathe. Fresh water in adequate supply must be available at all times. Horses who get most of their nutrition from hay, as opposed to being fed large amounts of concentrates, will require greater amounts of water to help them digest their food properly.

I am a firm believer in salt. I like the loose livestock salt as opposed to the solid salt block available for horses in most feed stores. If I feel my horses are not consuming enough free-choice salt, I will add one or two tablespoons of table salt to their grain several times a week.

> To get a picky horse to eat, feed it small amounts (a *handful* of hay or grain) once every hour rather than large amounts two or three times a day. To get a horse to drink on the trail, withhold water the night before a training ride (give a light feed when doing this), then ride a trail where you will encounter water within the first 10 miles, or have a friend meet you somewhere along the trail with water for your horse. Be prepared to wait until the horse drinks. Your horse will learn to drink when water is offered if it knows it cannot hurry home to water.

To utilize its feed, the horse's digestive system must be prepared to receive it. You can insure your horse's gastric juices are flowing by feeding it at the same time every day. That way its body is ready to digest the food when it gets to the stomach. I like to feed hay before I give concentrates for the same reason. When I feed whole oats (which is my base concentrate of choice), I soak them in hot water to break down the hulls (be sure to allow it to cool before giving it to the horse). Horses love soaked oats. Studies have shown endurance horses do well on a diet high in fat (rather than protein). A way to add fat to your horse's diet is by adding vegetable oil or rice bran. When I use rice bran I mix it with water, letting it range from sloppy (very wet) to mealy (slightly dryer). I feed it in a gruel state during rides. Corn has more fat and is more easily digested than oats, but should be fed at a reduced poundage when compared to oats.

All concentrates should be cut back at least 75 percent on the days when the horse does not work, more if they do not work for more than three days at a time. I do not feed concentrates when my horses don't work, except for a handful of rice bran in which I mix their vitamins.

Other feed stuffs used by many horsemen and women include beet pulp and (wheat) bran. Because it swells, beet pulp must be thoroughly soaked before being fed to a horse. Bran is also usually wet and served as a mash, especially after a hard workout. Before we leave the subject of feeding, let's not forget the goodies. Things like carrots and apples are often fed as treats, but they are also good food. I like to feed my horses five pounds of carrots each, several times a week, and I always include carrots in the food that is offered them at rides.

There are a ton of supplements for horses and if your pocketbook doesn't restrict you, it could be easy to overdo the supplement thing. Depending on whose advertising you believe, you can turn your horse into an overnight wonder just by feeding it their "right stuff." Of course it is never that easy in real life. If you want to experiment with different supplements to see how they affect your horse, use them one at a time, taking your horse off one before starting another. Keep a log of your horse's performance and allow from four to eight weeks to get a good feel for what, if anything, the new supplement or additive does for your horse and/or its performance. I try to stay pretty simple with my feed additives, using a multipurpose vitamin called Gold Dust (made by Big M Minerals). Gold Dust is moderately priced and has had a good track record through a variety of horses over a number of years with me. I also use a blood-builder supplement called Red Cell, which I feed only during the competitive season or when I am preparing a horse for a ride. Vitamins B1, B2, B3, B5, biotin, essential fatty acids, linoleic and oleic acid, nonessential fatty acids, lipoic acid, cartnitine, chromium, and amino acids ornithine alphaketoglutarate and creatine are all important to the efficient generation of energy, and so assume an important role in the diet of the endurance horse.

There are a variety of factors that will impact what and/or how much you feed your horse. They include age, amount of work, time of year, time of day and geographical location (what is available to you where you live and train). Any new feed stuff should be introduced gradually. Borrowing a little hay from your neighbors at a ride, or letting your horse eat strange feed provided by ride management at vet checks is something that happens frequently in the sport. But every time you change food stuffs abruptly, you run the risk of upsetting your horse's digestive system, which could lead to colic.

There is a saying: "A good feeding program is in the eye of the horseman." Anyone responsible for designing a feeding program and feeding a horse needs to note:

- Changes in weight

- Shine and texture of the coat

- Changes in attitude or energy level

- Color and texture of the manure

- Smell of the stall (amount of ammonia in the urine)

- Amount of water consumed

- Behaviors such as wood chewing, eating dirt or manure

- Changes in the hoof wall or texture of the hoof

SADDLES, BRIDLES AND HELPFUL GADGETS

The rules of the AERC, the governing body for endurance riding, don't mandate any particular type of saddle. Indeed, it doesn't require the use of a saddle at all. There are a variety of endurance saddles, many constructed on a western-style tree featuring a western-type stirrup with fenders but no horn. There are English (all-purpose, jumping and dressage) saddles, Australian saddles, western stock saddles and even treeless saddles.

What matters most in buying or finding a saddle for endurance is that the saddle fit both the horse and the rider, allowing them to do their jobs without interference. The size of the tree (length and width) and the angle at which it contacts the horse's back are what determines how well the saddle will fit the horse. The size and shape of the seat and where the stirrup hangs on the tree determines whether the saddle fits the rider comfortably. Most other design features are a matter of personal preference.

When considering the rider's needs in terms of saddle fit, think about the following:

- After it is placed on the horse's back, the saddle must offer a level place for the rider to balance (sit).

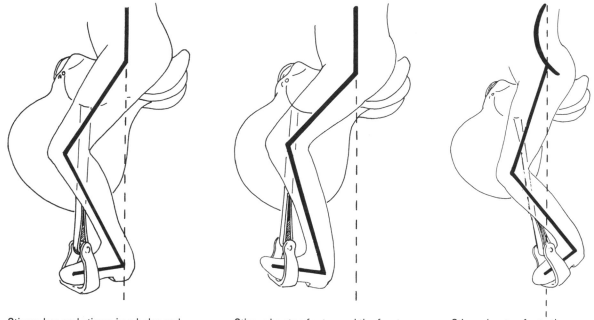

Stirrup bar and stirrup in a balanced position on the tree.

Stirrup bar too far toward the front of the saddle.

Stirrup bar too far to the rear of the saddle.

- A seat that slopes toward the horse's loins settles the rider against the cantle, encouraging a chair seat. The chair seat requires more muscular effort to maintain and is therefore an inefficient way to ride long distances.

- If the seat of the saddle slopes toward the withers, it causes the rider to unconsciously arch her back, thereby stressing the lower back.

- A stirrup attached to the saddle tree too far to the rear forces the rider's torso forward, encouraging her to lower her toes and lock her ankles. When this happens, the rider rides with all her back muscles tightened in a constant battle to rebalance her shoulders over her hips. A sore back or muscle cramps frequently results.

- A saddle that is too small in the seat can bruise the pubic arch, especially when the rider is trotting down hill.

Cordura (synthetic) Western Saddle by Big Horn.

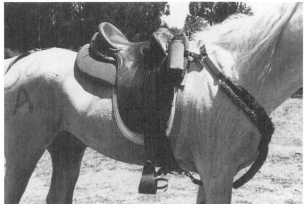

An Australian stock saddle without the horn.

Sharon Saare endurance saddle.

The Boz.

An English all-purpose model.

- If a saddle tree is too wide for the rider's pelvis, the rider will sit against the cantle with her knees pulled up in front of her in order to relieve the discomfort in her hip joints. This position puts the rider behind the horse's motion, resulting in muscle fatigue problems.

- A saddle whose stirrups are hung too far forward will also put a rider against the cantle of the saddle and contribute to soring the horse's back. Maintaining this chair-seat position requires increased effort from the rider during the posttrot.

- The wide fender usually seen on western-style saddles offers protection to a rider's leg, but can cause sore ankles for some riders.

- Narrow, English-style leathers swing more freely than their western counterparts, and are lighter in weight, but can also pinch the rider's calf and bruise her shins.

- Wide stirrups offer better support to the foot, but riders can get shin-splints if heavy stirrups cause their ankles to collapse outward.

- Narrow stirrups contribute to numb feet if the rider presses the balls of her feet against the stirrups for long periods of time.

- Stirrups with shock-absorbing devices help take some of the strain normally absorbed by the rider's knees. Caution should be taken when using them for the first time, however, if your heel cannot drop below your toe without causing discomfort.

Fitting the Horse

The first time a saddle is checked for fit, place it directly on your horse's back without pads. The gullet of the saddle must leave enough space so that no pressure is put on the spine. A space the width of three fingers must exist between the horse's withers and the pommel or fork of the saddle. If the gullet of the saddle is too narrow it will clear your horse's spine, but when you put your weight into the saddle, the narrow gullet channel will press on the edges of the long muscles of your horse's back on either side of his spine, pinching the edge of those muscles against the spinus processes and causing him discomfort. Most of the damage done by saddles that do not fit properly occurs deep in the horse's muscle tissue and can affect and radically change a horse's movement patterns long before surface symptoms such as white hair become visible. The angle of the saddle tree must match the angle of the horse's shoulder/rib cage. If a tree has too great a flair to the angle (too wide), the saddle will rest on the horse's withers causing bruising. If a tree is too upright in its angle (too narrow), the saddle will pinch the horse behind the shoulder. A tree with long bars on a short-backed horse gouges the horse behind the shoulders and in the area of the hip. A short tree on a long-backed horse can press on the loins, causing a sore back. If your choice is an English saddle, make sure it has wide panels to provide for good weight distribution. The panels on most standard English-type saddles are too narrow for distance riding. The cinch/girth must be attached to the saddle at a place that allows three to four fingers width between the horse's elbow and the cinch/girth when the saddle is set on the horse's back correctly (neither too far forward, nor too far back). After placing the saddle on the horse's back and before tightening the girth, the rider should be able to place his hand under the front of the saddle, palm down, with the tips of his fingers at the back edge of the shoulder blade, and run his hand down the horse's side under the front edge of the saddle without feeling the saddle bind his hand. You should be able to conduct the hand-slide test with equal ease when the girth is tightened and when you are sitting in the saddle.

You should also be able to slide your hand under the saddle tree along the horse's back for the full length of the saddle without encountering resistance or a pinched feeling with the cinch/girth loose. During the sliding-hand tree check, if your hand encounters a space under the saddle where the saddle fails to touch the top of your hand, the saddle is bridging. A saddle that bridges distributes the rider's weight only on the front and back edges of the tree. To check for a high spot in the panels or a twisted tree, put one hand on the right rear edge of the saddle and the other hand on the left front side of the saddle and press alternately. The saddle should sit solidly. If the saddle rocks, there is a problem with the fit. Reverse your hand position (left rear and right front) and run the same test. Dry spots, the appearance of white hair, wrinkled skin and bald patches or sheared hair (over the loin area) are all indications of a poorly fitting saddle.

Girths and cinches are made from a variety of materials, which include leather, plastic and various types of fabric. Horses have preferences in girth/cinch types. It is a wise rider who knows what her horse(s) likes and indulges him when possible. If the horse requires a breast collar and/or a crupper to keep the saddle in place on hilly terrain, use one.

Saddle-fit behavior problems include rearing, refusing to go forward, sluggish movement, bolting, jigging, rushing, refusing to stand when mounted, pinning the ears when saddled, kicking out when saddled, bloating when being girthed up, bucking, hollowing and dropping the loins and/or dropping the chest toward the ground when being saddled and pulling back when being girthed/cinched up.

Horse's backs are very different, just like people's feet. No one saddle "fits all." Even when you find a saddle that fits, you must be aware that your horse's back will change

- From the unmuscled, unfit back of a young horse to the more shaped back of the mature horse.

- From year to year depending upon the amount of riding and work the horse is receiving.

- From the beginning of a competitive season to the end of that season if the horse is turned out during winter months, or if his work is reduced and he is then campaigned hard during the spring, summer and fall.

- With muscular changes due to injury-enforced rest.

- With asymmetrical changes in muscling caused by unbalanced movement or physical discomfort.

Finding the right saddle is made more difficult by stores and saddle makers who want to limit the test period to a short ride in an arena. The endurance rider could be spending up to twenty-four continuous hours in a saddle on a 100-mile ride. If the saddle doesn't fit well, it will make the horse lame sooner (within the period of the ride) or later (two or three rides or years into the horse's competitive career). Plan on having a saddle for each horse you ride. Top competitors sometimes have a couple of different saddles for the same horse, using different ones at different times during a season, or even switching during a ride. Switching saddles is a way to insure the horse is only exposed to pressure points (of a particular saddle) for a limited amount of time. Of the most popular models of saddles used in endurance riding, I recommend the SR Enduro.

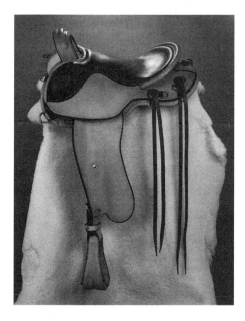

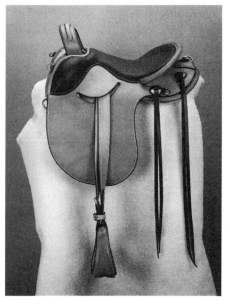

The SR Enduro.

The SR Enduro with flaps.

Custom-made by Steve Ray Gonzales of Bend, Oregon, the SR Enduro is exceptional in quality, and craftsmanship. There are three models, the Enduro (a western-type saddle), the Enduro with flaps, (offers an English-style flap and stirrup leathers), and a traditional English model. The saddle is custom-fitted, but can be restuffed to accommodate changes in a horse's back or a change of horses. It is also fitted to the rider. The stirrup-adjustment system eliminates the bulk common to western-style stirrup leathers, and the patented cinch attachment allows the cinch to be located anywhere from a 7/8 to a "center-fire" position. With a flexible fiberglass tree, the saddle is light-weight and has been thoughtfully designed to allow the rider freedom of movement and a balanced position regardless of gait or terrain. There is another plus: In a sport that is extremely hard on tack because of long hours of use and constant exposure to dirt, sweat and water, the SR saddles stand up exceptionally well. Finally, the saddle comes with a money-back guarantee.

Other popular brands of endurance saddles include:

- The Boz, a saddle that has a patented, flexible tree and a free-swinging stirrup, and seems to fit wide-backed horses well.

- The Sharon Saare, a western-style endurance saddle that offers a variety of tree widths.

- The Sports Saddle with no tree, which many people find comfortable.

- The Synergist, another western-style endurance saddle.

- The Big Horn Cordura, a synthetic saddle available in either a traditional western model with a horn or an endurance model with no horn.

- The Stübben Siegfried, an English saddle offering a great variety of tree widths and nine seat sizes. If you can find them, the old Siegfrieds made in Germany, are the very best, and fit a wide variety of horses' backs.

- The Albion by Mansion House, a saddle made specifically to fit women.

Expect to pay between $750.00 and $2,500.00 for an endurance saddle if you buy a new one. There are ways to stretch your dollars in this sport—sharing trailering expenses to rides, sleeping in a tent instead of buying a camper, using ice instead of buying ice boots—but when it comes to buying a saddle, buy the best quality saddle you can find that fits your needs and your horse. A saddle is only cheap if vet bills, delays in training and lost opportunities to ride don't cost you more in headaches and dollars than the amount you saved on the saddle purchase.

Used saddles are a good buy if they fit your horse well, are structurally sound (do not have a broken, warped, or twisted tree), and do not contain rotted or dry leather that could break at a critical moment, endangering your life. If you do find a saddle that fits you and your horse, *buy the one you have in your hand.* There is so much difference between one saddle and the next that even the same brand, style, seat size, tree, and manufacturer won't guarantee the saddle you receive will fit your horse as well as the one you have.

If the saddle is the type that has stuffed panels, you will need to restuff it perhaps as often as every six months and certainly once every two years if you put in many training and/or competitive miles. English saddles with foam panels can not be restuffed.

> A breast collar adjusted too high can reduce the horse's ability to breathe by pressing on its windpipe. One that is adjusted too tightly can prevent a horse from lowering its head comfortably to drink from a stream.

Pads

The variety of shapes, widths, types and sizes of pads is mind-numbing. A pad's primary purpose is to (1) protect the saddle from exposure to the salt and moisture of the horse's sweat and (2) protect the horse's back from a less-than-perfectly-fitting saddle. Not too long ago I attended a conference that featured a demonstration by Dr. Joyce Harman, an East Coast veterinarian who has done extensive research on saddle fit, using a pressure-sensitive pad and a computer printout showing pressure points by intensity. It was a thoroughly interesting presentation, but also somewhat depressing. Dr. Harman discovered most saddles are not symmetrical, even when new. Many times when various types of pads were added, instead of improving saddle fit, they actually made things worse! Finding the right pad or combination of pads is as personal as selecting your underwear. Best advice? Select three types that work (hopefully) equally well and rotate them. Pleasure riders can rotate once a week. Endurance riders should rotate pads every training ride, and once or twice during a competition. Each pad or set of pads focuses pressure a little differently. To do damage to the horse, pressure must reach a specific number of pounds per square inch for a specific length of time. By changing pads, you change the location and intensity of the pressure.

A horse with a sore back might need an orthopedic-style saddle pad such as the Saddle Right. While these pads are fairly expensive, they aren't as expensive as a new saddle and may buy you time so you don't have to choose between laying your horse off or continuing to risk injuring its back further, while you try to find a better-fitting saddle.

While wool or wool felt (not synthetic) is the best material to put next to your horse's back because it breaths, it is not easy to find, and it requires some extra effort to maintain it well. Rubber or rubberized products should never go against the horse's skin because they hold in heat and may scald the back. Gel pads dissipate shock but are heavy (good if you need the extra weight), and hold heat (they can cause a skin scald especially in hot, humid weather). Ulster makes a thin synthetic pad which breathes and is good if you only need to protect your saddle from your horse's sweat. Coolback and woolback pads by Toklat are well made, come in a variety of shapes and sizes, and hold up well. Care is needed in cleaning this type of pad or the fibers stick together in clumps after a while. These lumps can then irritate the horse's back. Try to have your pads conform as much as possible to the size of your saddle. Pads and saddles block heat dissipation, so you don't want to cover any more skin than is necessary with your pad choice. Pads that slip are a real pain, so ask around among friends before you settle on a particular type of pad if it is not already known to you. If the material feels slippery in your hand, chances are it will tend to slip under the saddle as well.

When washing pads, such as a one-inch wool felt pad, use a cold hose and a small brush, letting the sun and air be your dryer. If your pad can be washed in a machine, limit the amount of soap you use and be sure it is totally free of soap residue. To insure your pads are soap-free, run them through two cycles: one with and one without soap. Soap residue can cause a severe reaction in some horses with symptoms ranging from bumps on the skin, to inflamed, oozing sores. Pads should be cleaned once a month under heavy use and before a competition. The cost of pads will vary from about $50.00 to as high as $250.00, but price is no guarantee of suitability. Careful checking and observation of your horse and saddle fit is your only method of knowing for sure.

Bridles and Bits

While any type of head stall can be used in endurance riding, biothane is the material of choice. A plastic-covered nylon, the new generation of biothane is almost as pliable as leather, lasts a lot longer, cleans up with a dunking in a bucket of water, and comes in a wide array of great colors which make it fun to design your own color signature for your tack. I still love the smell of good bridle leather, but I wouldn't consider going back to leather headstalls or breast collars, because it takes so much time to properly care for leather that is exposed to the excessive water and sweat that are a part of the endurance game. A particularly popular headstall among endurance riders is the biothane halter headstall, which combines both the features of a halter and the features of a bridle. My personal choice is a western-style, single ear headstall that I can easily slip on and off over a halter. Go The Distance Biothane is a dealer known for quality materials and workmanship in its biothane tack.

While horses definitely have bit preferences, they pretty much respond to the various *types* of bits in a similar manner. A snaffle bit gives the greatest lateral control. A curb gives the greatest amount of braking power. If you use a strong bit in place of training, your horse will eventually become hard-mouthed and you will have nowhere to go to control him. Curbs, used too much, tend to cause a horse to tuck its chin into its chest. In that position it has a hard time seeing where it is going. They can also cause a horse to toss its

A snaffle bit gives greater lateral control.

A curb bit gives greater stopping power.

Some riders feel the device known as a mechanical hackamore makes it easier for the horse to eat and drink along the trail.

head excessively if a rider is heavyhanded or the bit or chin strap is adjusted too tightly.

A snaffle may not have the stopping power you need for safety during the early part of a ride, especially if your horse gets excited and strong, but there is no reason why you can't start with a stronger bit for more control and switch to a milder one once the horse has settled into its job and the edge is off. Mechanical hackamores are also popular with endurance riders. If you ride with a mechanical hackamore or a curb, use caution when your horse drinks from a watering trough, as the shank of your bit or mechanical hackamore can easily get hung up, making it hard for the horse to put his nose into the water to drink. There are a fair number of riders who use running martingales on their horses during a ride, but seldom have I ever seen a standing martingale (also known as a tiedown) and never have I seen draw reins.

In one catalog alone, there are fifty different choices of mouthpieces for curb bits, and two pages of different types of snaffles. What you put in your horse's mouth depends on your horse, his degree of excitability, his manners when in a ride environment, whether the shape of his soft pallet is shallow or arched, and his level of training. Generally speaking the thicker the mouthpiece in a snaffle, the milder the effect, but Arabians often have small muzzles (thus small mouths) and do not tolerate a thick snaffle very well. The longer the shank below the mouth piece on a curb, the more severe the bit and a snaffle and curb are distinguished, not by the type of mouthpiece but where the rein attaches/exerts pressure. A snaffle bit puts pressure directly on the horse's tongue, lips, and bars of the jaw. A curb bit puts pressure on the tongue, bars, chin groove (because of the chin strap) and poll of the horse.

I prefer a short-shanked curb with a jointed mouthpiece and a design that allows me to choose whether to attach my reins at a snaffle position, or at the end of shank in the curb position. That way I can change the strength of my bit by simply changing the position of the reins on the bit without having to change the bit in my horse's mouth.

Useful Gadgets

Heart Monitors A high-tech way of telling how hard your horse is working. The electrodes are attached to your horse in the area of the girth and under the saddle, and give the horse's pulse rate as a read-out on a watch worn on your wrist (or attached to the saddle or breast collar). When you first hook up your heart monitor, be sure to wet (soak) the horse in the area beneath the sensing surface to insure a good contact. Once you are on the road his sweat will insure a good connection and a good reading. The best on the market are the V-Max Equine Heart Rate Monitor System made by Equine Performance Technology in Reliance, Tennessee, and the Easy Rate Monitor made by Equine Performance Products in Pilot Hill, California. Cost is between $200.00 and $300.00.

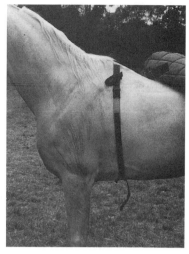

An on-board heart monitor offers an easy way to monitor the horse's heart rate.

Cool Offs   These innovative bits of cloth for the rider come disguised as scarves, shoulder ponchos and cap flaps, and for the horse as head coolers and shoulder coolers. They are, as the saying goes, "the cat's meow" on a hot day. They are designed to soak up water and retain it for several hours, helping to keep both horse and rider cool. Very reasonably priced, they are a must-have item on hot days. Available through Cool Off, Aptos, California. Cost is between $10.00 and $25.00.

Dura*Kold Ice Boots   The boots are reusable ice wraps in several different sizes, and provide cold therapy to any part of a horse's leg. The boots are easy to apply and remove and stand up to considerable punishment (being thrown around and stepped on). They can be cleaned by washing or hosing, and the panel design allows the horse mobility while receiving ice treatment. The ice pillow inserts stay in place while thawing and can be removed and placed in your freezer to chill. They are available from Dura*Kold Corp, Oklahoma City, Oklahoma. Cost is around $40.00 each.

Seat Savers   These saddle covers are made from dense sheep's wool and provide a wonderful cushion for rider's backside. Some models even cover the entire saddle. Cost is from $50.00 to $150.00.

Slip-on Sheepskin Pads for Stirrup Leathers   Made from merino sheepskin, these pads are for English saddles and attach over the stirrup leathers, providing comfort for the rider's leg. They are especially handy for the rider who wants to wear shorts, or for riders who ride English but don't want to wear half-chaps or tall boots to protect their legs. Cost is around $90.00.

Troxell Helmets An extremely lightweight, well-ventilated, ASTM/SEI-approved trail helmet. One of the best for trail riders, it not only helps protect the rider's head in the event of a fall, but also acts as protection from low-hanging tree branches. It comes with a detachable visor. Other lightweight helmets suitable for trail use include the Pro Lite and the Lexington. Cost is around $55.00.

The Troxell safety helmet is lightweight and well ventilated.

Snugpax A line of saddle bags designed to fit on the front or back of English, endurance or western saddles without bouncing. They include a variety of easy-to-access, zipper-closed pockets and places to put water bottles. Cost is around $50.00.

Bale Protector Bags A water-resistant bag to hold either a full or half bale of hay. Made of tough, indestructible materials and useful to keep hay from getting all over gear and equipment. Cost is $50.00 to $70.00.

Easy Boots A slip-on horse shoe of sorts, designed to help protect the horse's foot in the event of a thrown shoe. Some riders compete their horses in Easy Boots rather than shoes. They are also used over shoes for protection from pavement or rocky terrain. Cost is $35.00.

Collapsible Cart A great item to help carry necessary equipment into vet checks, this aluminum cart folds up to store in a very small space, yet has big wheels that roll easily over forest floors and grassy fields and can carry up to a 300-pound load. Cost is $200.00.

The Easy Boot is a must-have item when your horse loses a shoe on the trail.

Rump Rugs   A half-blanket affair that ties behind the saddle and lays over the hindquarters of the horse to keep the major muscles from chilling on cold rides or during windy checks. Cost is around $65.00

Sprayer Bottles   Carry one of these in your rider pack and spray yourself and your horse while you trot down the trail.

Water Bottles   An absolute necessity, they can be purchased at biking and running stores as well as in tack stores that cater to endurance riders.

Specialty stirrups   There are at least a half-dozen varieties of stirrups made especially for the endurance rider. Two popular styles are the shock-absorbing Trail Tech and the Cloud Nine. Lightweight with a wide base, costs vary from $50.00 to $100.00.

The list of specialty items continues to grow as innovative riders become entrepreneurs and start their own businesses around items that soon become as much a necessary part of the sport as the horse. What remains true in purchasing equipment of any kind is to do business with reputable merchandisers who know and test or will stand behind the products they sell. While manufacturers and retailers are obviously in business to make a living, their concern for the welfare of the horse and the safety of their customers cannot fall somewhere between zero and minus ten on their priority scale.

Sportack, a store and mail-order catalog headquartered in Walnut Creek, California, carries endurance-specific equestrian equipment. It is owned and operated by endurance rider Janeen Heath. Janeen's concern for her customers is evident in her friendly approach. She is always happy to answer questions and/or make suggestions to new riders, or get competitors' perspectives on the pros and cons of any of the merchandise she stocks.

6

Crewing the Endurance Event

A *crew* is a person or group of people who assist the horse and rider during a ride. The job of the crew is to arrive at the various vet checks or pit crew points along the trail with items that help the recovery of both the horse and rider. The need for a crew is impacted by the ride location, weather, comfort level desired by the rider, trail route, speed at which the rider intends to ride a particular event and the type or level of event in which the rider is entered. A local ride of 25 miles, consisting of two loops returning to base camp, can be easily managed without a crew. But no rider who has been selected to represent his or her country in the World Championships would consider attempting the 100-mile course without a support crew! Having a crew, however, is not a mandatory rule in the sport of endurance.

At international level events and tough hundreds (such as the Tevis), crews can consist of any number of people. Some are responsible for getting rigs to stops and running last-minute errands. It's great to have a massage therapist or TTEAM practitioner, a farrier, and a vet on your crew, as well as lots of hands for carrying things. I have been a part of a crew that consisted of all of the above and a person to work on *each* leg of the horse at vet checks—*plus* someone whose sole job it was to watch the heart-rate monitor as the pulse dropped and report the count to the head crew person. Ridiculous, perhaps.

Unusual, certainly—but the team was extremely well organized (with that many bodies running around it had to be); all members knew and performed their jobs with all the i's dotted and t's crossed and, as a consequence, the horses and riders for whom this crew were responsible lacked for absolutely nothing that could make their job easier or their recovery faster. I have also crewed four horses and their riders through a 50-mile ride by myself. While it is not an experience I care to repeat often, and my success in my role rested in the fact that all the riders stayed together during the ride and were riding horses who were all equally well conditioned, it nonetheless shows the scope of the possibilities and the impossibility of setting rigid guidelines about how many people are needed for a good crew.

Acting as a crew for someone is a big responsibility and shouldn't be taken lightly. The rider must be able to trust his or her crew, since it is largely the job of the crew to care for the horse during the period of time the horse and rider are in a *hold* or *vet check*. Correct care or the lack of it may be the determining factor in whether a horse and rider are allowed to continue or are pulled from a ride. A horse with an elevated temperature whose crew doesn't get him into the shade and cool him by sponging or spraying on water or a mixture of water and alcohol may fail to recover in the allotted time and be pulled. On the other hand, offering a hot horse cold water to drink, or allowing him to drink too much at one time, might result in stomach cramps (colic), muscle tremors, or push an already severely fatigued horse into collapse as it uses what little energy the body has left to warm the water in its stomach. Before agreeing to crew for someone, it would be advisable to attend an endurance ride and observe what happens there. Watch and learn. Many riders and crews are willing to answer questions if you ask them when they are not busy with other duties (there's usually plenty of time for this at vet checks while you are waiting for the riders to arrive). Observe how good riders and their crews do things. Crewing for a horse and rider during an event is very personal. Helping with the addition or removal of equipment needs to be done in a way which does not upset the athletes. A crew, be it one person or a group of people, needs to be ready at a moment's notice to abandon specific plans in an emergency, acting calmly and thoughtfully even when everything around them is chaos, as it often can be at hotly contested events, such as a World Championship. A crew in which each member is carrying a high degree of personal tension while performing his or her tasks may transmit that tension to the horse and/or rider. Horses are sensitive to tension and a tense crew can inhibit a sensitive horse from relaxing and recovering.

In addition to looking after the horse's basic needs, such as food, water and electrolytes, as a member of a crew you may have the responsibility of making sure your rider meets his or her basic needs as well. Many riders, even experienced ones, need prompting to eat and drink to replenish their energy and keep from getting dehydrated. Your rider may also want someone on the crew to supply her with information about changing trail or weather conditions, her position in the ride, approaching departure times (called "out" times) and the arrival or departure times of her nearest competitors. The list is endless and the more important the event, the greater the need for a well-rehearsed, experienced crew.

Crew members are often recruited from a rider's immediate family or friends. Endurance riding is a family event for some competitors, but when you're considering acting as crew for your loved one, remember your spouse may forget to say please and thank you under the stress of competition. If being ordered around and told you are (a) wrong, (b) too slow, (c) too late, (d) too fast, (e) too early upsets you, best to let the crewing scene to co-workers or less-attached friends if you want your marriage to stay intact. On the other hand, if you are romantically involved with someone whose obsession is the sport of endurance riding, there is no better way to test the depth of your commitment to your partner than to volunteer to crew. In the heat of battle, it can get pretty hairy!

PRIOR TO THE EVENT

- *Do a practice crewing with horse and rider before day of ride.*
- *Get specific directions to the ride location (base camp) from ride management.*
- *Safety-check your truck and trailer.*
- *Have a packing list and check everything twice.*

Crew members await the arrival of their rider at the 1996 World Championships in Kansas. Note the camp stove for heating water.

◄

If you decide crewing is your cup of tea, talk with your rider about her needs and specific strategy. Experienced riders often know just what they want done and will not hesitate to tell you in advance. While you're discussing what you hope to have happen, spend a little time playing a negative "what if" game so you have some idea of what may be expected of you if Murphy's Law takes over at the least convenient moment. For example, a thunderstorm poured buckets of cold rain on competitors and their horses prior to the prestigious Tevis Cup 100 Mile Ride in July, one year. Keeping horses warm and dry during the six to eight hours of bone-chilling downpour was nearly impossible. Who thought to bring waterproof blankets to a ride where 120-degree heat was expected? Twenty-five of the horses who spent the night shivering to generate heat tied-up early in the ride that year.

A loop trail is the easiest type of ride to crew and probably the best type of ride for a first event. On a loop trail, where the rider returns to base camp for the vet checks during the ride, the crew doesn't need to pack supplies, move camp, and set up a crewing spot in several different locations along the trail, and so is less likely to forget, lose or leave something important behind during the day. Both rider and crew are assured of having the necessary items—such as electrolytes, feed, water, etc.—which go a long way to provide a smooth, mishap-free first experience for everyone.

During holds (ranging from 15 to 60 minutes) the horse must be examined by a vet. Lines at vet checks can be long, making both the horse and

A crew member keeps food in front of her charge while horse and rider wait in the vetting line. ➤

rider wait. This leaves little time to do anything but the simple basics if you do not have a crew. The most difficult type of trail to ride without a crew to assist you is a straight-line route, where your beginning point and your ending point are often many miles apart. If you do find yourself riding such an event without a crew (I don't recommend it), you may be able to enlist a member of someone else's crew to drive your vehicle to the various stops along the route and to the finish line. Check with ride management to determine if they provide any form of transportation from the finish line back to your rig at the starting location, just in case you can't find a driver for your rig when you reach the ride site. If you are considering riding without a crew, you also need to know whether management will transport your horse back to your rig if you are pulled. Some rides leave it up to the rider and crew to get their horse back to camp if they are disqualified along the ride route.

When crew and rider have found each other, crew members should be prepared by going through a practice crewing. Discuss what to do, then select a predetermined crewing spot along the trail during a training ride. When the rider and the horse arrive, the crew should go through the motions as though they were on a real ride. This way both rider and crew get a feel for each other, and perhaps even more important, the crew gets a feel for their horse. The dry run is the time to make any necessary or desired adjustments in the crewing routine. During a training session, the rider won't feel pressured by the clock so she can take the time necessary to give her crew additional information calmly and with courtesy, asking them to fill water bottles, premix the electrolytes for her to carry to the next check where the crew won't be able to meet her, or put on the horse's Easy Boots for a rocky section of trail. On ride day you can expect everyone to be excited and even the most laid-back spouse/ friend may have a hard time staying calm especially if something goes wrong, like missing a marker and getting off trail, then arriving close to their cut-off time. If the crew knows exactly what is expected and how and in what order it should be done, it will be easier and more fun for everyone. A good crew is worth its weight in down sleeping bags, warm dry socks, horse shoes that stay put, and the best hot meal in town. Some members of a crew may get paid for their services—such as a massage therapist—but most volunteer their time, paying their own way for the privilege of putting in long hard hours for friends. It is customary for the rider to buy his or her crew a banquet ticket; moreover, it is considered good luck (positive thinking?) if you purchase your crew's banquet ticket when you mail in your ride entry. Ride management likes it too. It is also a nice gesture to give your crew a souvenir ride shirt, if ride shirts are available for purchase at the ride.

Often crew and rider travel together to a ride, either sharing a vehicle or driving in a caravan. Whether or not this is the case, crew need to know how to find the ride base camp. The best way to do this is to get specific directions, including landmarks, by calling the ride manager well before the ride. Ask for directions even if they are included as a part of your entry form; looking for landmarks in the dark is different than in the daytime. This is also the time to find out how far the base camp is from the nearest town, gas station, grocery store or motel. If you wait until the last minute to seek this information, the ride manager will be too busy to give specifics, "Is Laroou-Lerue-Lireau (spell it, please) where we turn, the dirt road with three *palm* trees, or the one with two *pine* trees?" Remember also, a day or two before the ride, the manager will probably be at the ride site unable to be reached by telephone. Most rides held in wilderness preserves or National Forests don't offer much in the way of a direct communication link. If you are planning to leave for the ride after work on a Friday and the nearest town to base camp is some small hamlet with one main street, you might also want to ask how late the stores are open. Establishments, including gas stations, in small towns tend to close early in the evening. Rigs that have two tanks and hold lots of gasoline can travel long distances between refueling. If this isn't the case with your vehicle, and you have to go miles off a main road to get to the ride location and use your truck the next day to crew the ride, you could find yourself running out of gas when you're headed home. There is nothing more frustrating than sitting beside the road with a tired horse and rider and an empty gas tank. Carrying an extra can or two of gas, several quarts of oil, jumper cables and the necessary equipment to change a tire on either your truck or trailer is recommended. The lugs on trailer tires are often a different size than the ones on car/truck tires, so be sure you have a lug wrench for *both*. With a "be prepared" attitude and good advance planning, you won't ruin your weekend (or your attitude) by missing a turn and having to drive miles out of your way on some narrow road because there's nowhere to turn around, or drive an additional 100 miles roundtrip to find gas, when you find the gas station in the closest town to the ride site closed at 7 P.M.

The drive to base camp can be an endurance adventure all its own, offering obstacles such as loose gravel, steep hills, dusty roads—with windshield wipers going full force, you *might* be able to see as far as your hood ornament, as you creep along at five mph behind a line of ten other trucks and trailers. Then there's the low-hanging branches challenge if you have a camper or an RV. Endurance riders are known for their perseverance, so I was not surprised when—driving into camp behind a rider who exemplified that spirit—I saw him mount up on the top of his camper with his chain saw as his wife drove their vehicle and clear the road of all the LHB obstacles for the rest of us with high rigs!

A safety check of the trailer and your towing vehicle are mandatory. Don't forget to check the simple stuff like oil and antifreeze. Trucks have been known to suck up antifreeze at an alarming rate if they are pulling heavy loads up steep hills on hot days in high altitude. Tires need to be in good condition, with the correct pressure. When checking tire pressure, don't forget to check the spares as well. Horses get touchy when asked to stand tied to the side of a trailer on the narrow shoulder of a super highway with eighteen-wheelers whizzing by at seventy miles per hour, so be sure to store your spare where you can reach it without being forced to unload all of your equipment or your horse. A handy little gizmo called a Trailer Aid, made of lightweight, high-strength polymer, is better than a jack for trailers. You simply place it under the wheel of the trailer and drive up onto it, which lifts the other wheel on the same side off the ground. I've used this device to change a tire without unloading the horses from the trailer. It is available through tack shops or catalogs and costs about $45.00.

Check trailer floorboards regularly and remember to get the wheel bearings repacked periodically. Check running lights, brakes, and the emergency brake system. If you have the fold-down feed doors on your trailer and travel with them open as some riders do, take a ride in your trailer to be sure your towing vehicle isn't enshrouding your horse in a cloud of carbon monoxide. Airflow paths around moving obstacles can be tricky.

The list of items and number of crew members needed will be determined by

- Your personal preferences and training routine, if you are riding. If you are crewing, the personal preferences and training routine of your individual rider.

- The place/speed at which the rider you are crewing plans to ride the ride (up front, middle of the pack or to finish).

- The type of event you are riding or crewing (figure one or two crew members per horse/rider at local rides, and don't be surprised to see seven or eight people per horse/rider team at major international events such as the World Championships).

- The location of the ride and number of entries.

- The ride route (loop trail, straight line, etc.).

- What services (hay, water, food for competitors, etc.) the ride management provides at checks.

- Anticipated weather conditions.

- The number of horse/rider teams you will be crewing, or that your crew will be crewing (an experienced crew person can crew two horse/rider teams fairly easily if the riders stay together during the ride).

- Your rider/crew housing accommodations (camper, motor home, tent, horse trailer).

- Your horse housing accommodations.

It is a mistake to assume that because you are bringing a camper or RV you will have all the comforts of home (including the kitchen sink if you need it) at any stop except base camp. Many vet checks have restricted access and it is often necessary to park up to a mile from the actual vetting/crewing area. In a "gate to a hold" type of check of 15 or 20 minutes, your rider doesn't have time to hike five minutes to a vehicle parked somewhere in a long line of other vehicles on an access road. Crews need to come prepared to carry to the crewing/ vet site all the supplies their horse and rider will need over distances of a mile or more (sometimes uphill) on foot! One of the easiest ways to accomplish this, besides having a family of lumberjacks or 200-pound bench-pressing weightlifters crewing for you, is a handy piece of equipment called a collapsible cart. Made of marine-grade aluminum, the end is removable and its hinged bottom folds upward, allowing the cart to be compressed to make it easy and space efficient to store and carry in your truck or trailer. Big wheels allow it to roll over most terrain and it can be used to carry saddles, water buckets and other items which could produce a hernia or at least a sore back by the end of the day.

This lightweight collapsible cart comes in handy for taking things from your vehicle to the crewing site. ➤

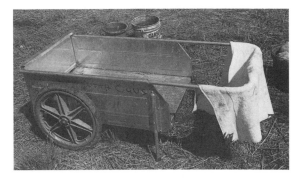

Following is a list of items that I have found useful when I have crewed horses and riders through the years. It is not complete because the individual nature of each horse and rider will cause the contents to vary. The lists also cover a wide range of competitive levels. A competitor in a local twenty-five mile ride will require less equipment, preparation, and planning than the rider and crew representing their country at an international event far from home.

RIDER LIST

Electrolytes   The human variety. Also, see the "Horse List" later in this chapter.

Water Bottles   These bottles are carried either on the rider's saddle or in a waist pack and are for the rider's drinking purposes on the trail, as well as for cooling the horse by pouring water on its neck.

Carry-All Packs   A connected series of padded pockets/pouches with places for at least two water bottles, these packs provide storage space for trail maps, glasses, sunscreen, food (such as energy bars/dried fruit/nuts), vet cards, and so forth. Packs are most commonly worn around the rider's waist or attached to the front or back of the saddle.

Fluids   Whether you carry water or some other beverage, the most important consideration is that you drink it. If you carry a drink because you have read that is the one to use or because someone else you know uses it, but you don't like its taste or it upsets your stomach, you may find yourself unconsciously avoiding drinking and will not rehydrate as you ride. This is a serious mistake. Dehydration can have negative effects on the rider's system as well as the horse's, so drinking continuously along the trail is important. Do not wait until you experience thirst before drinking. By the time your body has been deprived of fluids long enough to force you to drink, your judgment and/or motor skills may be impaired. One of the first signs of lack of adequate fluids is simply feeling tired. To this end, it is advisable to drink larger than normal amounts of water/fluids before the ride as well as during and after.

Food   Many riders do not want to eat during an event. Not eating will handicap both yourself and your horse. Your body needs fuel to do its work. The trick is to find something you like to eat that also provides you with the proper fuel for the job at hand. Most authorities agree that a high carbohydrate intake can best provide the ingredients necessary to keep your engine running throughout a ride. There are a number of ways to access such food, but the contents of the food is not the only consideration. Consider this scene: You have been on the trail for 45 miles. You are hungry, but when you try to eat that peanut butter sandwich your crew brought to the check for you, your stomach turns sour after the first mouthful. Worse yet, after you've forced yourself to eat half of the sandwich, you feel bloated and crampy! Not a good way to continue. Determining what food stuffs will suit your system during competition is just as important as being sure they are prepared and stored properly so they don't spoil. The best way to do this is through trial and error during training.

In addition to the horse and rider's food, the crew will need food for themselves. Simple, nutritional foods that are easy to store and carry are best and include fruit, nuts, yogurt, cold sandwiches (without condiments like mayonnaise, which may spoil), cold soup (store in Tupperware to insure no leaking), salty snack foods such as pretzels, a variety of drinks including plain water and soda and even some candy (sugar) for a quick energy pick-up when needed. If you are crewing a 100-mile ride, you may want some beverages that contain caffeine to help you stay awake, alert, and focused as the hands of the clock crawl towards 3 A.M. while you wait at a vet check for your horse and rider to appear out of the dark. If the weather is cold, a thermos of hot soup, cider or chocolate is a Godsend.

Light-weight folding chairs   Two is a nice number, one for the rider and one on which to place saddles, pads, and so forth, to keep them clean and free of dirt and irritating debris such as burrs or foxtails. They also come in handy for the crew while they wait for the rider to arrive.

Blankets   Handy for a variety of uses, from bedding for crew and rider on the night before the ride to extra warmth for the horse on a foggy, windy or rainy day. Use them at vet checks for the horse, crew and/or rider to prevent chilling, stiffening of tired muscles and stress from exposure. They can even be used as awnings on a hot day to provide shade, especially in an emergency.

Ice chests   Bring at least two, one for food and drink and the other for the horse's ice boots.

Extra clothing   For your own comfort you may want socks, T-shirt, windbreaker, riding pants, underpants, bra, and pantyhose. While the last two items may sound a bit strange, if you are a woman with a bust size over 32 and a bra strap breaks, you will be in a great deal of discomfort for the remainder of the ride (safety-pinning is not an option for fear of impaling). While riding tights are the best pants for this sport, if riding pants other than tights are worn, wearing pantyhose underneath can prevent or reduce clothing rubs for both men and women. The clothing you wear at an event should be something that fits well and is extremely comfortable, offering protection from such things as sunburn and/or windburn, poison oak or ivy scratches from brush or tree branches, ticks, and so forth. The way to know what wears and works well is to train in it. Don't wait until the day before a ride to replace your favorite pair of riding anything! An extra pair of shoes is also a good idea, especially if the ride may be visited by wet or cold weather. Cold, wet feet and an unprotected head are the best ways to chilling and fatigue and may contribute to hypothermia in an extreme situation (yes, endurance rides sometimes take place in snowy conditions). This is true for *both* the rider and the crew. Even when the weather is in a comfortable range, the rider's feet usually manage to get wet during the ride when they sponge or scoop water onto their horse. Changing into a dry pair of socks and shoes at the end of the ride day is a wonderful treat.

Personal toiletries   Typically such items include sunscreen, tissues, Band Aids of various sizes, moleskin, some antibiotic ointment, an ace bandage, the obvious female-specific equipment, plain aspirin or Bufferin, as well as an over-the-counter anti-inflammatory/pain reliever such as Motrin or Aleve, and insect repellent. Don't forget your antihistamine if you are subject to allergies from pollen (you may be comfortable at home, but traveling to a new geographical area with different airborne pollens could bring unexpected problems).

Flashlight or camp lantern (with extra batteries)   For those after-dark rider meetings and to find your way to the Porta-Potty in the middle of the night, you'll need some lighting. Having a flashlight also helps when you're trying to tack up before dawn.

An alarm clock   Most ride managers drive through camp on the morning of the ride, waking riders with a toot of the horn, but just in case you miss hearing it, an alarm clock will save your from the embarrassment of missing the start of the ride because you overslept.

A small emergency pack   This can be carried comfortably on your body and should contain a mylar blanket, small knife, waterproof matches, a whistle and a miniature flashlight.

Glow bars   You will want them if you are riding a 100-mile ride or know you will be on the trail after dark.

Horse List

Health certificate, Coggins test or passport   If you are crossing state lines or borders, or if any of these things are required by the ride management be sure they are up to date. See Appendix III for more specific information on horse passports.

Hay and grain   Bale bags are great for storing half or whole bales of hay without the mess. I save old grain sacks to separate and carry the grain I will need during a ride. Grain can also be premeasured and stored dry in buckets to be carried to the ride and/or crewing sites.

Electrolytes   While there are several different varieties on the market, the most popular brand with the best track record among experienced endurance riders is Endura-Lite, developed and tested by Dr. Jeannie Waldron, an endurance competitor and vet. You can get electrolytes through a local tack shop or animal health catalogs.

Water   When traveling from home, I bring water so the horses have familiar-tasting water to drink after their trip and before vetting in at the ride. If the trip is long or hot, they have a tendency to dehydrate. If they refuse to drink, or don't drink adequately during trailering or upon arrival because the water tastes or smells strange to them, they will start the ride in a state of dehydration. This will have a negative effect on their recovery and performance. Usually once the race has begun, even fussy horses will drink what is offered. For difficult cases, try regularly putting a little bit of apple cider vinegar in the water at home, then add it to their water at rides. The apple cider vinegar is good for them and it disguises the taste and smell of strange water. At vet checks water is needed for sponging and cooling, drinking, mixing with bran, wetting hay, and cleaning equipment (so it won't become abrasive), and your rider (for the same reason)! A cool, wet washcloth on a hot day is a wonderful pick-me-up, especially for a tired rider.

Buckets   Lots of them! Separate buckets are needed for watering, sponging and feeding. Remember the saying, "One can never be too rich or too thin?"

Well, in endurance riding the slogan goes, "One can never have too many buckets or too much water." Buckets are also handy for carrying small items like grooming tools, boots, straps, clean pads, Easy Boots, and so forth, to the vet check. Big, sturdy ones can be turned upside down when empty as a place to sit, or used as a mounting block.

Tack   Items include the horse's saddle and bridle, his saddle pad(s), his breast-plate if he uses one, as well as boots or any other special items such as a crup-per, which the horse is accustomed to wearing. It is a good idea to bring along extras, like reins, a stirrup leather, and a few miscellaneous straps for impro-vising if something breaks while on the trail. Extra saddle pads are a must (make sure they are clean and soap-free), and an extra cinch, or girth, as well. It wasn't too long ago I loaded my tack and horse into my trailer and hauled two hours to a trail head only to tack up and discover my saddle didn't have a cinch. The gal who helps me had taken it off to clean it and forgot to put it back on. It wasn't her fault I didn't check before leaving home and arrived without the necessary equipment!

A half dozen terry cloth towels   From bath to hand size.

Fitted Easy Boots   See Chapter 5 for more information about Easy Boots.

A water scoop or trail sponge   For cooling the horse on the trail. Scoops can be easily made by using old plastic Chlorox™ bottles with the bottom cut out.

Stethoscope   You need at least two: one for the rider (even if the rider is using a heart monitor) and at least one for the crew, plus wristwatches for both the rider and crew. The rider needs an ordinary watch because a digital wristwatch can interfere with the heart monitor receiver. The crew will find it easier to get a fast, accurate heart rate reading if they use a digital watch.

Heart monitor   A useful gadget known to go on strike occasionally. It moni-tors the horse's working heart rate with immediate feedback to the rider through a wristwatch type of receiver.

Grooming equipment   Be sure to include brushes, because you want to be able to present your horse looking his best the first time you or your rider makes it into the top ten! You will also need a sweat scraper, hoof pick, insect repellent, rubber bands and a long screw driver (it has a hundred uses in the hands of an imaginative crew, not the least of which is to help put on and take off Easy Boots).

Λ ride farrier all set up for business. ➤

Hoof Nippers   These work in a pinch as pullers to remove a shoe, nip a raised clinch or pull a nail. They can also trim a chipped or broken hoof, making fitting your Easy Boot in the case of a thrown shoe easier.

Although some rides have farriers in attendance, the AERC rules do not require one be there. The best thing is to be prepared. A shoeing hammer and clinchers are handy items to have along if you need to tighten the nails on a shoe and there's no farrier handy. Tightening a loose nail can keep a shoe from being thrown.

Vet Wrap   This is a disposable elastic wrap that can be used as a bandage or to support an injured leg.

Ice boots   The most popular kind are the Dura*Kold boots, which allow ice treatment without exposing the leg of the horse to water. They come in a variety of shapes and lengths to allow easy application to cannons, ankles and hocks. You can also apply cold therapy by using a shipping boot to hold crushed ice around the horse's leg, and by using products such as Instant Cold, which produces cold by a chemical reaction when the pouch is struck with the hand. Most boots, regardless of type, only give a good cold application for up to one half hour. After that they begin to lose their effect.

Rubbing alcohol   Added to sponging water, it causes more rapid evaporation and thus quicker cooling.

Electrolyte syringe   Unless you use a prepackaged type, a syringe of some sort is necessary to administer electrolytes to your horse. A 60cc-size syringe or larger is easiest to use and depress the plunger on.

Wound kit   A simple wound kit should contain sterile gauze pads of varying sizes, some form of mild antiseptic soap, a wound dressing such as Furox or Scarlet Oil, DMSO, small sharp scissors and either leg wrapping materials or disposable baby diapers (flat not fitted), which can be placed over a wound or used to apply pressure to stop bleeding.

Vaseline   An application to the back of your horse's pasterns before a race can help prevent overexposure to the drying effect of too much water. It also comes in handy for treating mild skin rubs in the girth area.

> Horses with white legs are particularly susceptible to a condition called "scratches" that feeds on moisture and sunlight. Once contracted, it can be very difficult to clear up and can inflame the skin in the pastern area during a ride, causing lameness.

Haynet(s)   Useful for feeding hay to horses who are tied up. Keeps horses from wasting their hay by walking on it.

Portable paddock equipment   If you plan to stable your horse at the event rather than tie him to the side of your trailer, you will need electric tape and charger or picket line equipment (a sturdy rope and ring).

Shovel, broom and manure fork   You'll need them for cleaning out the trailer and for picking up and bagging manure should the ride or the forest service require it.

Blanket(s) and cooler(s)   You will need these if the evening temperature drops, if your horse is clipped, or if the weather is cold or windy. Be sure your horse is used to wearing them *before* you put them on at the ride site. The best coolers I have found are made from Polarfleece, which allows moisture to escape while keeping the horse warm. Include a waterproof sheet as well.

Fitted set of horse shoes Have your farrier shape a front and hind set to your horse's foot. If your horse loses a shoe, the ride farrier, if one is available, only has to nail on the new shoe.

A sprayer is perfect for applying ➤
water to a horse on a hot ride.

Camping stove A small stove with plenty of propane can be used for heating water, cooking, and so forth.

Water sprayer A great type of cooling device, especially on hot rides; it sprays a mist of water.

Duct tape and string Duct tape is great for just about any type of emergency repair. Wrapped around the horse's hoof it helps insure your Easy Boots will stay in place. Sturdy string is good for tying things to the saddle or making repairs.

AT THE RIDE

Strictly speaking, crewing takes place during the ride, at vet checks. Official crewing duties do not usually include setting up base camp, but most crew are family or friends, so these duties could be shared with the rider or fall to the crew. When you arrive at the ride site, check with management to find out which areas are available for use and which will be reserved for use as a vetting area, if it isn't already obvious. Most ride managers/secretaries operate out of a camper or trailer. Look for a table, flags, a sign, or ask other participants where check-in is located. After you have determined where you are allowed to park, jump in and get busy if you know how your rider wants his or her camp laid out. If not, ask or wait. If it is not advisable to wait (for instance if it will be dark soon), lay out the camp in a logical manner. If you arrive before your rider, you may want to pick up your rider's rider packet and to save her standing in line. Checking the trail map (usually found in the rider packet) can help you find out if the trail is a loop trail, meaning you will be back at your present location during or after the ride. You will need this information to lay out camp. If you can't get the rider packet because your rider has failed to sign something, furnish management with the appropriate membership numbers or pay fees, ask to see a map of the course. You will need the vet card (also in the rider packet) to present the horse to the vet. If you are responsible for getting settled at the ride (let's say you hauled the horse while your rider is coming after work in a different vehicle), you may need to get the horse vetted before the rider arrives to comply with the advertised hours of vetting. If it falls to you to set up camp, review the tips in Chapter 7.

Upon arrival, after selecting a spot to make camp, unload the horse(s) from the trailer and check the horse thoroughly to make sure it was not injured during trailering. Include a jog out. If your rider is there, she will want to watch her horse as you do this. If you are alone, see if you can get someone to jog the horse so you can observe it. Riders sometimes want to vet-in their own horse if they are at the ride site early enough, or they may have you help them. In the case of multiple horses, your help is likely to be needed—and since you will be a team player with your rider and both of you will be responsible for the health and well-being of the horses in your care during the actual ride, it is advisable that you at least accompany the rider during the presentation of the horse so you can note anything about the horse that may impact your crewing duties the following day.

Delay vetting in immediately after arrival if time allows and let the horse settle down and accept its new surroundings. This will help your horse's heart rate, which has a tendency to elevate during trailering, to return to a resting rate. See that the horse drinks if possible so its hydration will be good. Getting the horse to eat will help keep its gut sounds active and walking or massaging out travel kinks will insure a good trot out. If your horse has traveled six or more hours to get to the ride, shows an elevated pulse or is dehydrated, he may manage to pass the vet check but certainly will not make a good impression on the examining veterinarian. A horse that stepped on itself in the trailer or is slightly crampy could be eliminated if presented immediately upon arrival, but may be fine with a little work. Time spent in preparation and examination of the horse before presenting it for vetting will give you the opportunity to catch and correct small problems before they become a negative note on your vet card, following you through the ride. A notation like "watch swelling on the right front" will make you anxious and can make vets feel they have to find something at other checks during the ride.

When camp is set up, and the horse has been vetted, watered, fed (I have found by allowing my horses to eat hay continuously throughout the night, they seem to have better gut sounds during the ride), electrolyted and settled for the night, it is time for rider and crew to sit down and go over the ride strategy for the following day. With a map of the trail, rider and crew need to decide which vet checks the crew will go to, what equipment and supplies will be needed/wanted at which checks, and whether the rider wants the crew to meet her any place along the trail other than designated checks. The temperature, topography, availability of water along the trail, and whether or not the crew will be allowed into all scheduled vet checks will be the determining factors in where the rider wants her crew to meet and assist her. At international events the crew is allowed to help its rider only at designated spots, but this is not the case in most rides. How many places the crew will be able to meet its rider depends on the layout of the trail, the type of roads the crew must negotiate in order to get to different points along the designated route and the pace at which the rider plans to ride. There are rides where crews must drive long distances to get to a specific checkpoint, while the rider goes cross-country "as the crow flies." If the rider is riding up front or going fast, the crew may have to leave before the rider actually starts the ride in order to be at the desired vet check before the horse and rider arrive. At Tevis, crews must travel to Auburn before being able to double back on a road that gets them into the first checkpoint at Robinson Flat (a trip of almost 100 miles for the crew and only 35 for the rider). If the distance is too great, the rider may want to split her crew (if the number of crew members, vehicles and supplies permit), sending teams to different stops to insure the crew arrives before the rider does at the checks.

If a crew must leave before its rider has started the ride, the rider and crew need to agree how long the crew should wait for the rider at a check. If the rider's horse ties up or goes lame a few miles into the ride, the rider may have to return to base camp rather than continuing on into the first check. She will want her crew to return to camp as soon as possible, bringing its rig. While telling your crew when to expect you at a particular vet check is always a good idea, the nature of the sport is such that you may not appear in that anticipated window. If this happens, good crew members will play detective to find out what has happened to their horse and rider before they make a decision to stay at the check or return to base camp. Detective work is easier if your rider or horse is wearing something noticeable. While a bright yellow saddle pad with shocking pink baseball-size polka dots may put the rider's color coordinating abilities in question, other riders along the trail will remember if and when they passed your rider and be able to tell you how far back on the trail she is. Pay attention to the riders who arrive just *before* your rider and riders who come in just *after* your rider at checks. It can help you decide if your rider is really late, or if the course just turned out to be longer/harder/hotter than anyone had anticipated and everyone has slowed down. If the latter is the case, usually a couple of riders both before and after your rider will remain in a similar relationship. If a few of those riders haven't come in, chances are your rider is fine. If ten or fifteen riders who were behind your rider leaving the last check are now in and there is still no sign of your rider, it's time to start asking questions and check with ride management, radio communications and/or other riders who have arrived. Be polite, but be persistent. Most rides have drag riders who ride at the tail end of a ride to be sure everyone has been accounted for, but there have been cases where a rider has missed a turn, or gotten off trail somehow and was missed by the drag riders.

Many rides provide a crew map, or at least directions to help crews find the vet checks. If this is not provided in the rider packet, ask for directions at the conclusion of the rider meeting and have a pen, some paper and a flashlight handy in order to write them down. Don't try to remember them. A wrong turn may make you late to a vet check. This could be only a slight inconvenience to your horse and rider, or it could mean a serious handicap for your team. After you and your rider discuss what you will need at what holds, recheck all your gear for the following day. If your rider packed, you will need to know where specific items are located in order to be sure to take them with you and/or know that you have them available. You may want to store things in groups in your crewing vehicle so you know that the stuff in the front seat must get to the first vet check, while the stuff in the trunk won't be needed until vet check three. You can use large plastic storage containers to organize the items that are needed at the different vet stops, then label the containers. If you should experience a delay, say a flat tire, send the appropriate container (mark all gear and equipment in an easily recognizable, permanent way) to the check with another crew. This way, essentials such as electrolytes are there when the horse and rider arrive even if the crew doesn't make it. These types of containers are available at general merchandise stores such as Sears or WalMart.

Attend the rider briefing. The crew needs to know the recovery criteria and may want to know trail information as well. If there are certain sections of the trail that are known to be boggy, dry, rocky, hot, and so forth, this information will influence what equipment or supplies your rider may want to have available or have extras of: for instance, Easy Boots and the implements for putting them on, adjusting them properly or taking them off quickly. While it is the rider's job to make these decisions, not all riders are cool, levelheaded thinkers the night before a big event (a *big* event for a rider can be his or her first 25/50/100 as easily as it can be a Championship ride). It may fall to you, the crew, to anticipate your rider's needs before your rider thinks of them, or before it is too late.

Somewhere between arrival, setting up camp, vetting in, having a strategy meeting, attending the rider briefing, taking care of the horse, and checking and preparing equipment and supplies for the following morning, the crew and rider must eat dinner. Some rides offer a catered meal (usually at an additional cost). If that is the case, it will be noted in the ride entry. While the cuisine may not be four stars, it is usually hot and filling and doesn't require any effort to prepare or clean up. If dinner is not provided by the ride and you have a camper or RV, you will have all the equipment you need for a good meal if you prepare food in advance and store it in Tupperware containers in your refrigerator or ice chest. Pop it in the oven or on the stove and the ride strategy meeting can be conducted around the table over dinner. If you are roughing it, sleeping in a tent or in your horse trailer, sandwiches that are prepared in advance and stored in an ice chest will work fine. Add wine if you wish and a cold pasta, along with some fruit or a fruit salad. Cookies for dessert will satisfy your sweet tooth. All of the above items can be prepared in advance, stored on ice in plastic containers and served on disposable dinnerware to save time, effort and trouble. Be a good camper and dispose of any trash in an acceptable manner. If the ride site doesn't provide a receptacle (most do), be prepared to carry your trash out with you. A box of big, heavy-duty trash bags is a valuable addition to your equipment list. Beside being used for trash or manure removal, trash bags make great emergency raincoats for rider and crew. Just cut slits in the side and top for your head and arms.

Some ride sites may require you to bag your manure before leaving. If this is not necessary, at least scatter it to help decomposition. The deer will usually devour any hay that is left behind. In some wilderness areas, nonnative seeds introduced in foreign food stuffs or horse's manure, are an ecological threat and a problem. Your ride entry should inform you if the ride is being held in a restricted wilderness area. If that is the case, you will be limited as to what you can bring with you and may need to switch feed in order to accommodate the rules. Be sure you do so well before the ride to avoid digestive upset in your horse.

Crewing the Ride

The specific procedures you follow to crew a horse at a vet check will depend on the following factors:

- The individual horse and its needs
- The desires of your rider
- The weather (heat, humidity, cold, rain, and so forth)
- The section of trail the horse and rider have just completed
- What the rider expects to encounter in the section of trail ahead
- The altitude
- The condition of the horse upon arrival
- The amount of time allowed for the hold
- The type of event in which the rider is competing
- The rider's current place in the ride and what place she would like to be in at the finish line

As you can see, this leaves a lot of room for variables from check-to-check, ride-to-ride and between horse and rider teams. When your rider arrives at a vet check, her horse will have to meet specific pulse and metabolic criteria before horse and rider are allowed to continue the ride. Metabolic criteria include

- Respiration.   Can be counted by placing the hand near the nostril or the flank of the horse; the normal resting rate is 12 to 20 breaths per minute.

- Heart rate.   Taken behind the left elbow with a stethoscope; normal resting rate should be between 28 and 44 beats per minute. The heart rate can be influenced by heat and humidity as well as stress and work.

- Capillary refill time.   Taken by pressing a thumb or finger against the horse's upper gum to blanch it, then counting the seconds it takes for the skin to regain its normal color; normal recovery should only take 1 to 2 seconds.

- Mucous membranes.   Membranes should be moist and pink in color.

- Jugular refill.   Taken by pressing on the jugular vein on the side of the neck, checking fill time; a dehydrated horse's blood is reduced and the vein takes longer to swell.

- Skin pinch test.   Done on the neck or shoulder of the horse; a one-inch fold of skin is gently squeezed together between thumb and first finger then released. The time it takes the skin to again lay flat is an indicator of dehydration level; normal recovery is immediate to one second.

- Gut sounds.   Taken with a stethoscope at the flank area on both sides. Reduced gut sounds are considered an indication of tiredness.

If a vet check is a "gate to a hold," it means the rider's hold time can not start until her horse's pulse is at or below the specified criteria announced before the ride at the rider briefing. If the rider is hoping to win or finish in the Top Ten, the amount of time spent in getting her horse to reach criteria is critical. Let's say two horses arrive at a check together. Horse A's crew goes to work and horse A recovers to criteria in five minutes. Horse B on the other hand, takes ten minutes to recover to acceptable criteria. Rider A has just gained a five-minute lead on his competitor, plus rider A's horse didn't have to do any work to get that lead. Now rider A will be released five minutes before rider B may once again start.

If the vet check is a straight hold of a certain time period, rather than a "gate," all riders have the same amount of time to get their horses to an acceptable pulse (and respiration) before presenting them to the vet. If a horse fails to recover to the required criteria during the hold time, the vets can either assign an additional time penalty or eliminate the horse and rider from the ride entirely. Some rides assign a time penalty if the rider or crew presents a horse to the vet with a heart rate that has not stabilized at or below criteria (usually 60 to 64 beats per minute). These penalties add time to the "hold" and can run from 10 to 30 minutes. Because penalties are to be avoided for obvious reasons, the rider and crew should be careful not to rush their horse into a vet check too soon. If the ride is using the Cardiac Recovery Index test as a part of the process for determining the horse's fitness to continue, extra care must be taken by the crew to insure the horse is stabilized below the mandatory pulse criteria before presenting, or the horse may be eliminated.

> The CRI or Cardiac Recovery Index is a test where the horse's heart rate is taken, after which the horse is trotted out and back (a distance of 125 feet) by the rider or crew. Exactly one minute from when the horse begins the trot, the horse's pulse is checked again. If the pulse stays the same or is lower, all is well. If it rises only one beat, the vets will probably allow the horse to continue if all other criteria seem normal. If the horse's pulse fails to recover sufficiently, it is considered a sign the horse is suffering from exhaustion or pain and it will be pulled.

If your horse and rider are simply riding for a finish, they can stay as long as they like in the vet check after passing the vet exam, as long as they remain within the ride's cutoff time limit. A little extra time at a check often pays enormous dividends when the horse and rider are back on the trail, so as long as your rider isn't front-running you can take a little extra time to insure the horse is well recovered before leaving the vet check. An exception to that philosophy might be if the vet check is at night and/or the weather is very cold or windy. In either case, prolonged standing around—especially without a protective cooling sheet and/or blanket—may cause the horse's muscles to stiffen up, making the horse appear lame. In cold or windy weather, it is better for the horse to move *slowly* along the trail as soon as it is allowed to leave the check, rather than stay at the check exposed to the elements. If the horse is pulled or the rider must remain in the check longer than normal, blanket the horse with a cooler and walk it slowly, allowing it to stop and eat or drink every few minutes as it desires.

A horse's pulse recovery rate will depend on the horse's condition, whether or not he is experiencing any pain or discomfort (lameness, bruising, muscle tie-up, tack rubs, and so forth), his internal temperature and his electrolyte balance, as well as the surrounding temperature and atmospheric conditions. A hot horse with a high pulse rate, for instance, standing in direct sun on a hot, humid day will have a much harder time dissipating his performance heat and therefore his pulse will drop more slowly than the same horse under the same stress on a day when the temperature is in the seventies and the air is dry. His recovery rate will also depend on how hard he has been ridden just prior to arriving at the check. A horse ridden well within his fitness parameters will arrive with only a moderately accelerated heart rate and will recover quickly (generally within 5 to 10 minutes). A horse pushed into extensive anaerobic work (work without the benefit of oxygen) will have a high heart rate that will be slower to return to normal. A horse that takes longer than 10 minutes to recover is probably being pushed too hard. Be sure to let your rider know how long it took her horse to recover, if for some reason she does not stay with the horse while it is recovering. Be sure you get the rider's vet card if she leaves the area; you will need it to get your P&R (pulse and respiration) time and take the horse to be vetted.

In most circumstances, the job of getting the horse's pulse rate below ride criteria should be the crew's first priority. When the crew arrives at the vet stop, locate the water source and decide where the best spot will be for your horse and rider when they arrive at the stop. If the ride is expected to be hot, look for a shady spot, remembering you may have to share a tree with another crew (there are roughly four sides to a tree). If you arrive at 10 A.M. and stake your claim to the shady spot at that time of day, and your rider doesn't arrive until 2 P.M., the shade and the cooling advantage it offers may be somewhere else. In a crowded vet check, ridiculous as it may sound, staking out and monitoring your crewing/parking/camping spot can become important. If someone's horse is disruptive (kicks, uses aggressive body language, and so forth), or is allowed to walk through your camp and over your horse's hay or supplies, your horse and rider will suffer for it. Even the best-intentioned rider may have trouble keeping his hungry/thirsty horse from sticking its nose into your horse's feed or water bucket if it is too close to them. While a small bite or sip is seldom a big deal, a spilled bucket of sun-heated water that you carried a half mile uphill is an expensive loss. Experienced crews use various devices (chairs, buckets, bodies) to stake out their crewing spot. If a horse runs backwards while his electrolytes are being administered, and bumps into your horse who is just starting to urinate, causing him to stop and then refuse to urinate, you will realize how important it is for your horse to have space in order to relax and recover. Most crews and riders exhibit a cooperative attitude and attempt to share what space is available, especially if the crewing area is crowded. As crew, it is your responsibility to see that your horse and rider have what they need.

Whether you want to be close to the vetting area or away from it depends on how your horse and rider handle activity. Sometimes even having a choice in the matter depends on when you arrive at the vet check. At some rides, vet checks may have limited access and conditions can be very crowded, especially if the check is a short one. A horse and rider can lose precious recovery time if forced to walk a half mile to their rig before the crew can begin its job. No matter where you set up, if you are not clearly and obviously in your rider's line of sight as they come into the check, one of the crew needs to stay by the in-timer or trail until your rider arrives, so no time is lost while the rider hunts for you. If the horse refuses to rest if it can see other horses being trotted back and forth for the vet, you will have to set up your crewing area a little farther away from the main activity of the stop. A notable aspect of a really top-class endurance horse is its ability to tune out all the commotion surrounding it at vet checks and simply get on with the business of eating, drinking and resting.

Tailgate crewing.

No matter where you set up your crewing site, you will probably have to tote water and your crewing supplies. Only occasionally can you simply drive to where you are going to crew, open the tailgate of your truck or the back door of your camper and crew from it.

When you get your water and crew supplies to the crew site, if you do not have a camp stove to heat water, set your water in the sun to take the chill off.

To help the horse recover, the crew needs to get lots of water onto and into the horse—especially if temperatures are above 80°F. and the air is humid. Some horses have a preference in the temperature of their drinking water. Knowing what that preference is may help you entice your horse to drink more. Another way of getting water into the horse during holds is to soak hay and offer a sloppy bran mash.

A hungry horse dives into his bran mash at a lunch stop.

Avoid putting cold water on the large muscles of the hindquarters of a hot horse. Cooling these muscles too fast can cause cramping. Water can be safely applied to the head (just behind the ears), neck, shoulders, legs (especially the inside of the legs where veins are large and close to the surface), under the belly, and ribs. Once the water has been applied, use the side of your hand or a sweat scraper to remove it as it becomes warmed from the body heat, then reapply more cool water. Most riders believe in using cold water. I have found, contrary to popular opinion, that cool/tepid water is best. Horses cool by heat transference; their body heat transfers into the cold water. Ice-cold water applied to hot skin shrinks the tiny capillaries that carry the blood to the surface, where they interact with the air for the cooling process. When the capillaries become constricted, the surface (skin) temperature appears to drop significantly—but cooling of the core temperature is slowed, since not as much blood can reach the surface of the skin through the restricted-capillary supply line. Tepid water can be safely applied to the back (when the saddle is removed) and the hindquarters without undue risk of muscle cramping. To increase the rate of evaporation (the process actually responsible for carrying heat away from the horse's body), add one pint of rubbing alcohol to your bucket of sponging water). Take care to insure the alcohol water does not get near the horse's face or eyes.

> • *Alcohol added to sponging water helps speed the evaporation of the water from the skin of the horse, increasing the water's cooling effects.*
>
> • *Removing the saddle can speed cooling and pulse recovery.*
>
> • *When removing the saddle and pads place them where they will not pick up burrs, foxtails, sticks, leaves, dirt, and so forth. Picking foxtails or burrs out of a fuzzy fabric is very time consuming.*

Remove the saddle, if time allows. The additional cooling afforded by exposure of the horse's back to the air and sponging can help drop the horse's pulse more rapidly. There is also a psychological impact. In most instances, when the horse experiences having its saddle removed, it is at the end of its work period and signals to the horse's system that a rest period is coming. Once mentally conditioned to this state, a horse is more prepared to rest and relax when its saddle is removed.

Getting the horse into a shady spot for crewing, especially on a hot day is another method of getting a quick pulse recovery.

No trees for shade? No problem, this crew brought its own.

◄

Since there is no guarantee of a shady spot at the crewing site, some riders and crews use portable, lightweight awnings to provide shade for the horse at checks. Water can be sponged or sprayed on the horse. When sponging, a big sponge (carwash size, not dishwashing size) works best. Natural sponges, although more expensive, harder to find in large sizes, and less stable than synthetic ones, hold more water than commercially manufactured ones. While crews are not allowed to work on the horse during the actual vetting process, a large bath towel can be soaked with ice water and placed over the horse's neck during the vetting procedure, further cooling the horse and protecting it from the sun.

A wet towel draped over the horse's neck helps cool him and provides protection from the heat of the sun during vetting. ➤

TTEAM work on the accupressure points of the horse's ears has been shown to lower the pulse rate. (See Chapter 4 for a detailed description of TTEAM.) It is best if the horse is familiar with this type of work before trying the technique during the ride. Some riders administer additional electrolytes to help lower a pulse that is hanging too high, provided that the horse is drinking well.

When the weather is cool to cold, the crew must maintain the horse's temperature level by using coolers and blankets. The pulse of a tired horse that is cooled too fast or allowed to chill drops more slowly and may not drop to its normal rate at all. Massage keeps blood flowing to the tired muscles (helping to carry away toxins created during work) and keeps the horse from stiffening or cramping. While it is always a question whether to let the horse rest and eat, or to walk it occasionally to insure muscles do not stiffen, what you do must depend on what you see before you. If the horse is well within its parameters, let the animal eat and rest, while doing body work on it. If it is tired and shows signs of stiffening (such as an altered gait or a reluctance to move), use massage and then move it around slowly for a short period of time (3 to 5 minutes) every 15 or 20 minutes during the hold. This is especially recommended if the hold is an hour and occurs toward the end of the ride and/or at night. Carry some hay with you and allow your horse to nibble on it as you walk so the horse can get as much food into its system as possible. While the length of the horse's digestive process prevents food consumed during the ride from providing energy for the ride effort, it will help maintain gut sounds (one of the metabolic measuring sticks used by ride vets in determining a horse's fitness to continue) and, equally important, it gives the horse a mental boost.

The application of moist heat is a secret for keeping a horse comfortable at competitions in cold weather or at night. Soak thick terry towels in hot water (as hot as you can stand to put your hands into) and apply them to the horse's hindquarters and shoulders; cover everything with a blanket or wool cooler to keep in the heat. Change the towels, replacing them with fresh, hot ones, as soon as they begin to cool. Moist heat and massage keeps the muscles from stiffening up from the cold. Remove the blanket and hot towels just before your rider leaves the stop.

The rider may want you to ice her horse's legs at checks, especially if they are traveling fast. When using ice or ice boots, apply for 20 minutes, then remove for 10 to 15 minutes. Reapply as necessary if the leg needs further cooling. While you are working on the horse's legs, check to make sure all the shoes are still tight and that clinches have not risen. A risen clinch on the inside of the hoof can gash the opposite leg. Check for simple things too, such as stones wedged in a shoe.

As a crew member, you should be familiar with the stethoscope and how to use it to check your horse's heart rate. If you do not have a stethoscope for some reason (you forgot it at the trailer), there are P & R people at each check who are responsible for officially recording your horse's pulse and respiration on your vet card. This must be done before the horse is presented to the vets for its metabolic and soundness exam. If they are not swamped with work, the P & R folks are usually willing to give you a courtesy (unofficial) reading on your horse. With practice, you can learn to feel your horse's heartbeat with your hand at several places on the body including, (1) under the jaw, (2) behind the knee, and (3) in the lower leg. When time is extremely important, it is necessary to keep a constant check on the horse's dropping heart rate until it reaches criteria.

In addition to adjusting and/or maintaining the horse's body temperature at optimum level, the horse needs to be offered food stuffs. Hay and grain are normal, but if grass is available it is much the better feed since it contains a lot of water. Dry hays retain only small quantities of water in their makeup. When allowing your horse access to grass, you need to use some judgment as to the length of the grazing time. During vet checks there is probably not enough time for the horse to overindulge in grass consumption; but prior to and after the ride your horse may colic if it has not been receiving alfalfa or had any previous exposure to green grass and is allowed to graze all night long. First-time grass encounters should be limited to 15–20 minutes, no matter what your horse tries to tell you about his preferences. Your rider will tell you in advance what food to bring to the various checks for the horse.

The horse's electrolytes will also need to be administered before it leaves the stop. If the electrolytes are administered as soon as the horse arrives, it may provoke the horse to drink more before it leaves the hold, especially at one-hour checks. Some horses do not like electrolytes and will not eat after they have been dosed. If this is the case with your horse, do not administer the electrolytes until just before the horse and rider leave the check. One internationally famous competitor feels that the salts in electrolytes upset her horse's stomach, so she mixes the electrolytes with Maalox and seems satisfied with the results. Electrolytes are usually administered by mouth with a large syringe (60 cc or larger).

The easiest way to insure that your horse gets the necessary amount of electrolytes is to administer them by squirting them into his mouth with a large syringe. ➤

I have found that by mixing them with baby food (such as strained carrots or applesauce), horses seem more willing to take them without a fuss. Give electrolytes during training to accustom the horse to accepting the syringing procedure. If the horse is exceptionally resistant to getting his electrolytes, put only the baby carrots or applesauce in his mouth during training. He'll get used to the idea of it being something good and be less resistant to accepting his electrolytes during a ride. Of course he'll know you've added something the first time you dose him at a ride, but by the time he gets over expecting to like what he's getting, the ride will be almost over and you can go back to dosing him with straight applesauce again. Beyond lowering the horse's pulse, cooling the horse (or keeping it warm), feeding it, attending to tack (removal, change and resaddling), presenting it for the vet exam and trot out, checking and adjusting auxiliary equipment like boots or heart monitors, scoops, sponges, Easy Boots, etc. and administering the necessary electrolytes, an experienced crew can use TTEAM work and massage to make the horse more comfortable.

While it is best if the horse urinates along the trail when it feels the need, many horses will not do so. Encourage the horse to urinate during the hold by taking him to a grassy spot (some horses do not like to splash their own feet and will not urinate if standing on hard ground). A way that sometimes works to get a horse to urinate is to allow your horse to smell the area where another horse just finished urinating. When your horse urinates, watch the color of the urine. It should be clear and yellow. Slightly cloudy toward the end of the stream is still OK, but dark, coffee-colored urine is a danger sign and needs to be called to the attention of your rider and the vet. If your horse passes manure, notice if the manure is normal or dry. If the horse is dehydrated and its manure is dry you need to get the horse to drink before trailering home, or you run an increased risk of impaction. Some riders feed wet bran throughout the ride.

Once a horse and rider have entered the hold, the horse's pulse has dropped and the rider's hold time has officially started, the horse can be presented to the vet anytime up to the stated time limit. You may wish to take the horse directly to the vet after its pulse has dropped, rather than waiting the full amount of the allowed time before presenting. This is especially true on 100-mile rides, when the horse and rider have 80 or more miles behind them and it is dark and cold. Even a sound horse left standing too long may stiffen up in these circumstances. It is a good rule of thumb to get the horse through its vetting as soon as possible upon arrival.

The following signs indicate that a horse is experiencing discomfort or approaching exhaustion:

- *Lack of interest in food or water.*

- *Slow capillary refill time.*

- *Sustained high pulse rate or respiration rate.*

- *Thumps. This term refers to a synchronous diaphragmatic flutter seen as a "twitching" in the flank area of the horse. It is thought to indicate an electrolyte imbalance.*

- *Restlessness or constant pawing, especially at food or water.*

- *Unwillingness to move freely forward once on the trail (a lot of horses resent being trotted for the vet during their rest period, so reluctance to move forward during the trot out may not be an accurate indicator of your horse's fitness to continue).*

- *Slowing down on hills.*

- *When a horse that is ordinarily a balanced mover travels on its forehand.*

- *Stumbling.*

- *Lack of gut sounds.*

- *Muscle tremors.*

- *Refusing to take a certain lead in canter.*

- *Loss of interest in surroundings or food.*

- *Refusal to urinate or coffee-colored urine.*

- *Eye appears worried, dull or glazed.*

A crew member should observe the vetting. Watching the horse trot can be revealing. If the rider is presenting the horse and trusts your eye, he or she will undoubtedly want to know what your impressions were, especially if the vet feels there might be some slight abnormality. Vets are human and fallible. Some horses move in strange ways. If the preride vet doesn't pick up the movement anomaly and note it on the vet card, the horse's unusual way of going may be questioned later on in the ride. It is not good for your rider to be anxious about the soundness of his or her horse. That type of tension promotes premature fatigue. Unless you are sure the horse is off, try to make the rider feel confident. If the vet thinks the horse is lame, he will pull it, so if the horse passes, your job is to help your rider continue the ride without nagging pictures of disaster. Your ears can detect uneven foot strikes or a loosening shoe when the horse is walked or trotted on hard ground or pavement. Listen to him as you lead him around. When you arrive at a vet check, find out if there is a farrier on hand and where he is located so you can find him quickly if your horse needs to have a nail tightened or a shoe replaced.

If you are the one to trot the horse for the vet, give the horse enough lead rope to allow it to carry its head straight. If you pull the horse's head and neck toward you when it is moving, it unbalances the horse and can make it appear to be lame. Some riders/crew have learned to hold the halter tightly, forcing the horse's head to stay up while trotting it out. This can be attributed to simple ignorance on the part of the handler, or it can be an attempt to disguise an uneven way of going. Most vets today are experienced enough to recognize such tactics for what they are and will instruct the handler to trot the horse again giving it greater freedom of its head and neck. They may also do this if they feel the horse's trot out was compromised because the horse cantered or jumped around in an uncontrolled manner. Long-strided movement and good impulsion is normally a plus and scores an A on the vet card under impulsion and attitude. A short, shuffling trot, however, with no animation calls less attention to any unevenness in stride. If you think you might need to use this strategy at some point in the ride, show the horse in the shorter gait at the preride vet check so his way of going remains consistent throughout the ride, or the difference will be noted and become cause for concern. If you minimize a horse's potential weakness during a check, you must realize that you may not have won the game but instead may be putting your horse in serious jeopardy. Long miles of remote wilderness between vet checks are not the place you want your horse to crash metabolically or to go seriously lame. A long walk home at best—or a tragic loss of your partner at worst—could result.

While there are many functions a crew can perform to help its horse and rider recover quickly, one of the most important things a crew member needs to do is *look* at the horse and really *see* it—particularly when the horse and rider arrive, and then periodically during the hold. Start by looking the horse in the eye. What does it show? Is it calm, bright, and eager, or anxious (pain?), dull, or exhausted? Now look at the whole horse. What is the horse saying with its body language? Is it comfortable and relaxed or tense and nervous?

Are the belly or flank muscles rigid? Does it point one foot (stone bruise?) or shift its weight from one leg to the other frequently while standing? Constant shifting can signal a range of problems, ranging from gut pain to muscle fatigue to limb discomfort. The tail should be relaxed, not clamped tightly against the body—a symptom that indicates chilling or discomfort. Do the legs have interference marks, fresh cuts, scrapes or scalded skin that require additional attention? Are there any hot spots on the legs or in the saddle area? Determine this by laying the palm of your hand lightly on these areas and moving it slowly while evaluating the heat difference. If you think you feel a spot that seems warm but are not sure, check the other leg or the other side of the back in the same area and compare temperatures. Hot spots are early warning signs of pressure or internal breakdown. If you flex the leg at the knee and run your fingers down the tendons at the back of the cannon bone with a little bit of pressure (watch the vet do it at the preride check or get your vet at home to show you how it is done), does the horse show discomfort repeatedly at the same spot on the leg? After the horse has cooled down and his coat is dry, does he sweat in patches? Is the horse's back visibly wrinkled, scalded, irritated or rubbed in any area? How about behind the elbows or in the area of the girth? A little bit of vaseline can help keep a skin irritation from worsening. Good crew members see all of the horse even while they are focused on immediate needs and duties.

After the horse and rider cross the finish line, they must pass one more vet check (the recheck) in order to officially complete the ride. Usually the recheck is held one hour after the horse and rider finish. The criteria is "fit to continue." If your horse stiffens up, is lame, or its P & R doesn't recover to acceptable rates, your horse and rider could still be pulled, even after crossing the finish line. Crewing duties, therefore, don't stop until horse and rider are cleared by the vets at recheck and the horse is cooled, rested and fit to be trailered home safely. Since the horse is still in competition until after the final recheck, no liniments or poultices can be applied to the legs or body until after that time. Ice is recommended instead. Massage is allowed and used by the smart competitor and crew. Combine rest with lots of water, using the same guidelines as you did at other vet checks. Once the horse has passed the final vet, it must be cooled out, allowing the internal temperature to return to normal. Make sure water consumption stays up by continuing to wet food stuffs and to offer fresh water. A body brace such as vetrolin can be applied in a sponge bath if the weather is warm after the final vetting. Cover the horse with a cooling sheet while it dries, unless it is sunny and hot. Walk it slowly or tie the horse in the sun to keep it from chilling. When your horse is dry and cool, whether or not you were able to rinse it, give it a good brushing and check the feet and legs for cuts or abrasions one last time. I apply support wraps to my horse's front legs after a ride. If there is any question in my mind, I will apply a poultice to pull heat as soon as I get home. If the horse has worked hard and is a little stiff, I give one tablet of bute (I take aspirin the day after, too) and massage the large muscles before I load the horse to haul it home, then do stretching exercises with it and massage it the following day.

If your rider has finished among the first ten riders, the horse will be eligible for the Best Condition award. More on preparing a horse for Best Condition judging can be found in Chapter 7.

Crewing the Rider

Trying to crew both horse and rider is a difficult job. Oftentimes at big events, a crew will have at least two people, one to care primarily for the horse and the other to help the rider. The rider needs to eat and drink at checks. Unless she feels completely at ease knowing the horse is being properly cared for, she will not do so. Try to position your rider where she can eat and rest while being able to observe what is going on or being done to her horse. This way she can conduct the proceedings without jumping up every few seconds to do something the crew should be doing. Getting a rider to eat may be harder than you think. Adrenaline, nerves and sometimes general fatigue all work together to suppress the appetite. Fatigue can be brought on simply by lack of water. To allow a rider to leave a check at night, well into a 100-mile ride, having neither eaten nor drunk can mean impaired judgment and pathfinding skills. If the rider doesn't like what is put in front of her, she will have to be extremely disciplined to eat. Your rider will probably provide her own food and your only responsibilities will be to see that it gets to the appropriate stops and to put it in her hand. You may also want to take the gentle but persuasive stance of staying around until you see them finish the meal. Dried fruit and nuts are good to tuck in your rider's trail pouch, so they can munch small amounts frequently on the trail as they ride. Energy/nutrient bars as well as candy can be carried for an energy boost. The Ironman Triathlon Bar, available in stores catering to runners, is based on the recommended 40/30/30 ration, 40% of the calories from carbohydrates, 30% from fat and 30% from proteins, and comes in three flavors. Drinking is even more important. Most riders will drink, but not enough. Make sure water bottles are refreshed at each check and if your rider uses a special sports drink, be sure she has a supply of it as well as water. Be ready with extra clothing in case something rubs, curls/pulls up, breaks, gets wet, gets lost or gets torn. Dry socks are especially appreciated and beneficial, as is something to keep the rider's head warm if the weather is chilly or cold. If the weather is hot the rider will peel off layers and leave them with you, but it is advisable to keep them at hand if the ride is a 100-miler. The rider may want them again when it cools off at night. Getting the rider to sit or lie down if the hold time permits it is a great idea, even if it is only for ten minutes. During this time you can massage the rider's neck and shoulders or her feet. Using small handheld hot packs (that get hot when you activate a chemical reaction in the pack, and so do not require boiling water or an external method of being heated) on stiff or achy muscles of the back and legs is especially effective. Ice packs around the neck, face and forehead are refreshing on a hot day. You can also use them to treat a sprain or swelling or abrasion. If the weather is chilly, be sure your rider stays warm when she is resting. She will be warm when she climbs off the horse, so she will probably not want to put anything on; however just like the horse, riders can quickly become chilled, when they stand or sit around during a check. Working the outside edge of the ear is a way to warm someone and is also a good treatment for shock in people as well as horses. I always carry some Bach's Rescue Remedy with me. It has an array of applications, from nausea to lightheadedness, and can be used for both people and animals. If it is hot and the rider seems disoriented in any way, be sure she takes both electrolytes *and* a salt tablet. Since riders can tell you what they are feeling and what they need, it *should* be easy to help them; but in the heat of competition not all riders are aware of what they need or that they must care for themselves, and some do not feel comfortable asking for things. Constant attention and friendly reminding is the way to help the rider do and be his or her best.

If you disagree with your rider over any particular issue, try to work around your differences for the duration of the ride. If your rider gets upset, you two can talk it out when the ride is over and the pressure is off. Most riders are very appreciative of their crews and the attention and care they get during a ride. The job of crewing is not for everyone, but can be a fun experience. The scenery, the companionship with other crews and riders, the excitement and/or peace (depending on where in the ride your rider is running and the level of event) is all a part of the experience.

It's Ride Time

Whether it is your first ride ever or one ride in a season's schedule, call or write for the entry well in advance (Tevis often fills up months ahead) and mail your completed entry form and check to the ride secretary several weeks before the ride. Some rides allow entries at the ride, but if you plan to do this call and check with the ride manager in advance. Entry fees vary across the country and from event to event, averaging $60.00–$75.00 per horse and rider at local events, and as much as $275.00 per horse and rider for special high-profile events such as the Tevis and the Race Of Champions. Your ride entry will inform you of any additional fees necessary, such as park fees. Trailering across state lines or borders and competing in international events requires additional expenses. You will need documentation of a negative Coggins test and/or a health certificate. For international competitions, you will need a horse passport (see Appendix III, "Passporting Your Horse for International Competitions"). Plan ahead to allow time for lab work if these items are needed.

Trailering to the Ride

If your ride site is just around the corner and your horse is used to being trailered, you won't have to think about much to prepare for this stage of an event. If your ride is 2000 miles away, however, you have a lot of planning to do. You will need rest stops every four to six hours. Pull your vehicle off the road and get a cup of coffee while you let your horse's legs rest from road vibrations. Every eight to ten hours, you will need to stop where it is safe to unload your horse and walk him around for 20 minutes or so. Letting your horse graze in places that are manicured, such as a rest stop, is a health risk. Vegetation can contain weed killers or other chemicals. Offer water each time you stop. Some horses are reluctant to urinate while moving; which is another reason to take breaks. Most horses I've hauled prefer a slant-load stock-type trailer. I think they like the constant supply of fresh air, and being able to see out and identify the strange sounds around them. A slant-load is less wearing on muscles.

To tie or not to tie may be the question, but it is not one that I will answer. Whether you tie your horse in the trailer or not is up to you and the behavior of your horse. Most trailers have dividers that make it difficult for a horse to turn around or get into too much mischief, but I have seen horses get their bodies into some incredible positions in very small spaces. Technically speaking, I've never actually *witnessed* the double-jointed contortions that *had* to have taken place for my horse to end up the way I once found him when I opened the trailer door—they only do things like that in secret so we never know the true extent of their athletic prowess. But because I've had horses lift a divider right out of its pegs, causing it to fall to the floor between their feet, I tie my horses.

Horses hate dividers that go all the way to the floor. It prevents them from spreading their feet to balance themselves. I know more than one horse who started the bad habit of scrambling because of a solid divider. Fortunately few trailers are made with solid dividers anymore, but if your trailer is an older model and has one, I'd recommend having it cut in half, lengthwise, before you spend a lot of time hauling your horse around in it. If bad weather is a factor where you live, but you want a stock-type trailer, get Plexiglas inserts to keep out wind and rain. The new fold-down feed doors are great, but allowing the horses' heads to hang out of them while traveling isn't something I recommend. The new aluminum trailers are so well made as to be almost watertight, but in the summer the temperature inside can get uncomfortably high very quickly. Be aware of this situation and check your trailer periodically during a haul. If you must haul through desert or extreme heat, try to plan your trip so you can drive through the hottest part of the route after dark.

Thick mats act as shock absorbers, but it is a good idea to have some drain holes drilled into fitted mats (and the trailer floor) to provide a quick exit for urine. Shavings provide cushioning but also absorb urine, holding ammonia fumes in the trailer. If you are hauling long distances and have dividers you can adjust to allow wider spaces between horses, it is best to give them as much space as your trailer and your load allows. Horses ride better with more room. The overall height of the trailer must be high enough to enable the horse to carry his head and neck at a comfortable angle and to let him feel at ease when he approaches the trailer and prepares to step in.

Time spent at home to trailer-condition your horse will pay big dividends by reducing travel stress for you both. It will also help reduce the chance of physical injury, which is greatly increased if there is a struggle to get your horse to load, or if the horse engages in prolonged pawing or kicking once on board. When loading your horse, have a helper shut the rear door, stall divider or butt chain before you tie the horse in. Most trail riders I know don't wrap their horse's legs for trailering to a ride the way show people often do and most horses arrive just fine. Leg wraps won't hurt, however, if your horse tends to step on himself or the horse next to him in the trailer (you also probably need to slow your driving speed a bit, especially around corners). Introduce the horse to the leg wraps before you are ready to load him into the trailer. Some horses stomp or kick the first time they have wraps applied, especially on their hind legs.

Experiment with hauling your horse in different places in the trailer. Horses have preferences—whether because of vibration or noise, I don't know—I've hauled enough horses enough miles, however, to know that put in a front slot one horse will scramble and perspire, but put in the back slot the same horse will ride just fine. My motto in this regard has become don't argue with success, just find out what keeps them happy!

> To become more aware of what your horse experiences when hauled in a straight-load trailer versus a slantload, stand with your feet slightly apart and have someone push you from the front or back. Notice how much muscle tension you have to use to keep your balance, especially if you have to keep your feet together. With your feet hips width apart, have that person push against your shoulder from the side. You'll see how much less effort it takes to balance yourself against disruptive force from a lateral direction.

Setting Up Camp

When you arrive at the ride site, unload your horse and check him thoroughly; include a jog out to make sure he weathered the trip in good condition. Offer water and hay. Have your crew walk the horse around to take the kinks out, especially if the horse has been in the trailer for more than two to three hours. A little body massage and some stretching exercises will help the horse relax and limber up before being presented to the vet. Check in with the ride secretary, pick up your rider packet, and ask about the time and place of the rider meeting. If you have time, delay taking your horse to the vet until it has had time to drink and eat a little. To set up your camp in an efficient manner, you'll need to answer some questions. Will your camp (or vehicles) need to be moved before the end of the ride? If you will be returning to camp and expect hot weather, you may want to position your trailer to make shade available for your horse after the ride. If it is 10 A.M. when you choose your camping spot, you may need to think ahead to have shade the next day when you finish at 2 P.M. The opposite will apply if you expect cool or cold weather. You will want your horse to be able to take advantage of the sun's warmth to keep from chilling during the postride care period.

If you are hauling your horse 500 miles or more, try to arrive a day early in order to allow your horse to recover from the trip. If you live at a low altitude and are competing at a high altitude, you want to arrive as close to the ride as possible without unduly tiring your horse or else allow a couple of weeks for the horse to acclimatize. Most riders choose to arrive just before the event because of job and family commitments.

Arriving early at base camp lets you pick a good spot with room to set up your portable corral (if you plan to use one) or get your pick of parking spots. Park close to a good tree(s) in order to rig a picket line. Picket lines can be run from one tree to another, from a tree to a trailer, or between a trailer and a motor home or camper if they have the appropriate hardware solidly bolted to them for tying a line safely and securely. Factor the location of the water and possibly the toilet facilities into your site selection. Being close to the road can mean lots of dust and noise as other competitors arrive. Level ground is best, but sometimes hard to find. Unless you're a bat, the next best thing is to sleep with your head uphill. If you have a camper or RV and plan to use your appliances, you may need to level it after you park before your appliances will work.

An aluminum slantload gooseneck trailer with living quarters, and a roof rack for carrying additional items such as hay. ➤

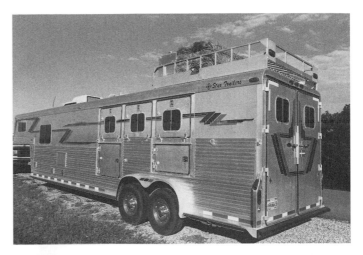

A trailer showing how portable panels are frequently stored and carried. ◄

A high-sided, stock-type, bumper-pull trailer used as a place to tie the horse. Note hay bag, water tub (large), feed pan and two buckets with water for sponging. ➤

A portable corral set up and ready for the horse.
◄

Two types of containment corrals: on the left, a portable corral from PVC pipe; on the right, an electric (tape) corral. ➤

Try to find a reasonably level spot for your horse as well. If you are planning a campfire for cooking or just to enjoy as a part of the outdoor experience, be sure to check with management to see what the restrictions are. Beware of tying horses directly under trees or in tall grass, as doing so can quickly result in a tick infestation. A heavy application of an insect repellent (look for one that repels ticks as well as other insects) especially to the legs as soon as you unload the horse from the trailer, will help protect your horse from these little bloodsuckers.

If all the vet checks are not back at base camp (and they seldom are), your crew may need to use your vehicle. Plan your camp so you can take whatever equipment you will want or need without disrupting the entire camp—especially if you will be returning to your original camp site at the finish of the ride. If your crew will need your truck, don't park it facing into the woods with your corrals set around your trailer, or you'll have to tear everything down in the morning before your crew can get the truck out to go to your first check. If space is tight, pay attention to where you are going to set up your paddocks or tie your horse. You don't want your porta-corrals so close to your neighbor's that the horses can reach each other (or worse yet, each other's food), nor do you want horses tied to trailers so close together that the horses can kick each other.

This can mean two horses tied to the one side of a trailer, or it can mean two trailers—each with a horse tied to it—parked close together. Even if your horse is normally a mild-mannered Clark Kent type, it could unexpectedly exhibit aggressive behavior if an unfamiliar horse gets too close to its food or a companion.

Experienced riders often head off just such a situation by setting out a few chairs at the perimeters of the space they need until their next-door neighbor arrives and settles in. No one wants to tear down a camp after it is already set

A smart rider has escape-proofed this stallion by securing him with a wide nylon neck collar that is attached to the trailer by a separate rope, in addition to the horse's normal halter. ➤

up, only to move his or her horse 20 feet or so. Setting out chairs or buckets is also a way to save space next to you if you are expecting a friend to arrive later in the day.

Endurance riders use a wide range of camping accommodations, including sleeping bags on the floor of the trailer. Most accommodations depend on the rider's sense of adventure, desired comfort level and size of budget.

If you are using a paddock to stable your horse, be sure the individual panels are secured to each other firmly and attach the whole unit to either your trailer or a tree. Many paddocks are made of PVC-type pipe, and even the metal ones are lightweight. Neither will provide any significant containment to a horse that becomes nervous or excited. Paddocks constructed of electrical tape are also common. The tape is run through holding rods stuck in the ground and a charger is attached. This type of setup allows great variety in the size and shape of the paddock, but be sure your horses have experience in an electrical-tape paddock at home before putting them in one at a ride. Also, don't make the mistake of making the paddock so small that if the horse accidentally bumps into the tape and gets shocked, he bolts through the other side.

If you are going to turn two horses out together in the same pen and intend to feed them together without tying them up, you better be absolutely certain they are good friends and will share their food or they may kick or bite each other. Kicks can be serious. Bites usually aren't, but if one horse bites the other in the saddle area and your spouse can't put a saddle on his or her horse the following morning, all will not be well.

If you do not have a paddock, you can tie your horse to the side of your trailer. Make sure the lead rope is tied only long enough to allow your horse to reach the ground with its nose, otherwise it may get hung up in its rope. Hang hay nets high for the same reason. Secure water buckets so that the horse can't upset them and end up going without water all night long.

Being familiar with poisonous plants that might exist in the geographical area of the ride is an extra measure of protection for your horse. A very good book to help you quickly identify toxic plants is the *Horse Owner's Field Guide to Toxic Plants* (Breakthrough Publications).

Sleeping bags on the trailer floor—an economical way to camp. ➤

Many riders spend the night before a ride in a tent. ➤

This camper mounted on a flat-bed truck offers all the comforts of home, plus lots of additional storage space and big truck power for hauling. ➤

THE VET-IN

This is the first impression the ride vets have of your horse. You will need your vet card (in your rider packet) in order to get your horse vetted. Put the card in a plastic bag to protect it during the ride. Vet lines can get long at big rides, so come prepared. When standing in line, don't become so involved in chatting with your neighbor that you fail to notice your horse is about to kick the horse standing next to you. If it is your horse that is being threatened in that manner, you will want to move it out of harms way.

At some rides your horse's pulse and respiration will be taken and recorded on your vet card by a P & R volunteer before you present your horse to the vet. The purpose of the preride vet check is for the vet to determine whether your horse is fit and sound enough to start the ride. A vet (there could be one, or as many as a dozen if the ride is a major, well-attended event) will examine your horse, noting his/her metabolic criteria on your vet card.

A vet checks the capillary refill on a horse.
◄

Listening for gut sounds. ➤

RIDE NAME _____ **DATE** _____ **DISTANCE** _____ **Rider #** [ ]

Rider Name _____ Weight Division _____ Junior Rider [ ]

Sponsor's Name (Juniors) _____

Horse Name _____ Age _____ Breed _____ Sex _____ Color _____

RIGHT SIDE — LEFT SIDE

Mark at points of concern (can use contrasting color at final exam)

Pre Ride (First) Examination		Post Ride (Final) Examination	
P _____		P _____	
R _____		R _____	
T _____		T _____	

Post Ride Final: Heart Rate _____ Recovery Index _____

Parameter	ABCD	Comments	Parameter	ABCD	Comments
Muc.Memb.			Muc.Memb.		
Cap Refill			Cap Refill		
Jugular Refill			Jugular Refill		
Skin Tenting			Skin Tenting		
Gut Sounds			Gut Sounds		
Anal Tone			Anal Tone		
Muscle Tone			Muscle Tone		
BackWithers			BackWithers		
Tack Galls			Tack Galls		
			Wounds		
Gait			Gait		
Impulsion			Impulsion		
Attitude			Attitude		
Overall Impression			Overall Impression		

Signature of Examiner _____

Elimination Reason _____

Signature of Examiner _____

Signature _____

Vet check #7

TIME ARR TIME	# 7	NAME OF STOP		MILEAGE

	P/R	PARA	A,B,C,D	Comments
P/R Time		Muc.Memb.		
		Cap Refill		
		Jug Refill		
Recheck #1 Time		Skin Tenting		
		Gut		
		Anal Tone		
Recheck #2 Time		Muscle Tone		
		BackWithers		
		Tack Galls		
Out Time		Wounds		
		Gait		
		Impulsion		
Heart Rate Recovery Index		Attitude		
#1				
		Overall Impression		
#2 (Recheck)				Examiner

Vet check #8

TIME ARR TIME	# 8	NAME OF STOP		MILEAGE

	P/R	PARA	A,B,C,D	Comments
P/R Time		Muc.Memb.		
		Cap Refill		
		Jug Refill		
Recheck #1 Time		Skin Tenting		
		Gut		
		Anal Tone		
Recheck #2 Time		Muscle Tone		
		BackWithers		
		Tack Galls		
Out Time		Wounds		
		Gait		
		Impulsion		
Heart Rate Recovery Index		Attitude		
#1				
		Overall Impression		
#2 (Recheck)				Examiner

A rider vet card. Areas for vet-check information from checks 1 through 6 appear on the back of the card.

These criteria include (1) the color and appearance of the mucus membranes, (2) the capillary-refill time, (3) the jugular refill time, (4) the skin-tenting response (to determine the horse's state of hydration), and (5) the gut sounds. The vet will also score your horse's muscle tone, and anal tone, and will examine the back, withers, girth area, and legs for any sign of soreness, swelling or abrasions. It is a good idea to have even old injury marks noted on your card so your horse is not penalized later for something that was present before you started.

When the vet has done all this, you will be asked to trot the horse out and back so his soundness can be observed. Many times the trot out will be held in a field with less than desirable (to anybody) footing. Try to pick the best footing possible when you trot your horse out. Give the horse as much length in the lead rope as you can and still have him behave himself and stay in gait. Try to trot straight away from the vet, then stop to turn the horse and trot back. Don't ask the horse to trot a tight bending line at the end of your trot out, especially if the ground is uneven. If the vet wants to see you circle the horse as a part of the preride exam, he or she will tell you so. If this is the case, trot your horse on a large circle, again stopping to change direction. Any horse turned tightly or abruptly in either direction on unlevel footing is liable to put in an uneven step or two. Experienced vets ignore it, but I have seen vets, new to the sport and unsure of how picky they should be, make too much of this type of a misstep. If unfounded, the opinion may be overruled by a more experienced vet or the head vet, but seldom is it overruled without a note on the vet card, which then follows the horse and rider through the ride. Having that notation on the card can cause the most experienced riders to worry and doubt their own judgment about their horse's soundness. It also tends to make other vets look harder and wonder if they should be finding something wrong. A preride score also is given by the vet on gait, impulsion, attitude and overall impression, and any abnormalities, cuts, splints, etc. on the horse are noted on an outline figure of a horse on your vet card.

After your vetting is completed and the card signed by the vet, it will be returned to you. It is your official starting pass and you will need to show it to someone in the area of the vetting to get your horse numbered. Keep the card with you throughout the ride. You will need to present it at every vet check.

Riders who participate in the sport in a specific region, or nationally, quickly get to know many of the vets who work endurance rides, and it is just as common to have a preference of personalities and procedures at a ride as it is in private. If you find yourself with a horse who moves a little weirdly, and there is a vet at the ride who knows your horse has completed five 100-milers this year, all in good condition and all with the same unusual way of going from beginning to end, get into that vet's line at any vet check you can. If there is only one line and riders who are next in line take their horse to which ever vet is available, move your horse back in line a space or two until the vet you want is available, then walk your horse to that vet. There may be times when you are front-running and will not want to sacrifice the time; other times you will not care. It is not cheating in any way, however, to present your horse to the vet whose judgment you trust the most and who best knows your particular horse, or who has the greatest amount of experience with the demands of the sport and the peculiarities of its athletes.

RIDER BRIEFING

The evening before the ride, there will be a rider briefing. Since many rider briefings take place after dark, I recommend you take a flashlight, folding chair, a pen, some paper and your *ride map*. The ride map, also called the trail map, will be included in your rider packet.

It is here you will get your starting times (50-milers usually start before 25-mile riders), specific up-to-the-minute trail information that will include the color of the ribbons or other type of marking devices on various portions of the trail, where the start is located, where you can expect water along the trail, at which checks or where along the trail your crew may meet and assist you, the recovery criteria for the ride, the type and length of each vet check—for example, straight hold, gate to a hold, trot by, and so forth—and information such as whether the vets want the saddles pulled before the horse is presented to be checked. Your vet card is the best place to note recovery criteria for each check, since it must stay with you throughout the ride.

If you are smart, you will mark trail information on your trail map and keep it with you during the ride. Your crew should attend the meeting with you. Any questions you may have about the trail or the vet-check criteria will be answered by the head vet or ride management at this meeting. If you are confused about something, now is the time to ask (you'd probably be surprised how many other riders are sitting out there with the same question as yours). When the meeting is done, it's time to go back to your camp, do one last run-through of the equipment you will need first thing in the morning—such as electrolytes, water bottles filled and waiting, water buckets filled in advance (if you are on a loop trail and will return to camp at some point during the ride, etc.)—check that your horse has adequate amounts of hay and water before you turn in, give him a preride dose of electrolytes, set your alarm and crawl into bed.

The Start

Rides can range from 15 to 250 entries. As you may imagine, it makes quite a difference at the start if you are starting with 250 other horses all fit to do a 50- or 100-mile distance. Many rides have what is called a *shotgun start.* Riders assemble in a specific location and start simultaneously. A sale day at Macy's with everything in the store priced at $1.00 would have nothing on this rush, especially if you're in the middle of this sea of horses. You can't expect to be buried among a hundred trotting horses and have your horse walk. You also can't expect your horse to take a sedate trot if the horses around him are hitting a 14-mile-per-hour lick, so be prepared. Your best defense at the start of a ride is to put your horse with the group you think will pace the way you plan to. Admittedly this is hard to do if you are on your first few rides, since it takes a little exposure to the sport to get to know riders in your area and begin to learn who rides where and how fast they go. Asking won't help much. Most endurance riders, if asked, will say they don't go fast, but one person's slow is another rider's land-speed record. Riders who know they are going to ride strongly throughout the ride usually gather in the front of the pack and move out first. Those who are riding to finish hang back in the crowd letting the "go-fasters" (as they're sometimes called) get on down the trail. Most rides permit riders to start up to 15 minutes after the start time, so if your horse is young, inexperienced, or difficult to handle in a crowd, and you don't believe in the philosophy of "letting him get it out of his system by running the first ten miles to take the edge off," it is a good idea to wait and start after the rush. Anyone planning to start in trot should warm their horse up for ten minutes at walk before they come to the starting line. You can do this mounted if your horse is quiet, or you can do it in hand, to avoid having to fight with him once in the saddle. Being herd animals and instinct-driven, it takes some time and concentrated training to get horses, especially Arabians, to be willing to

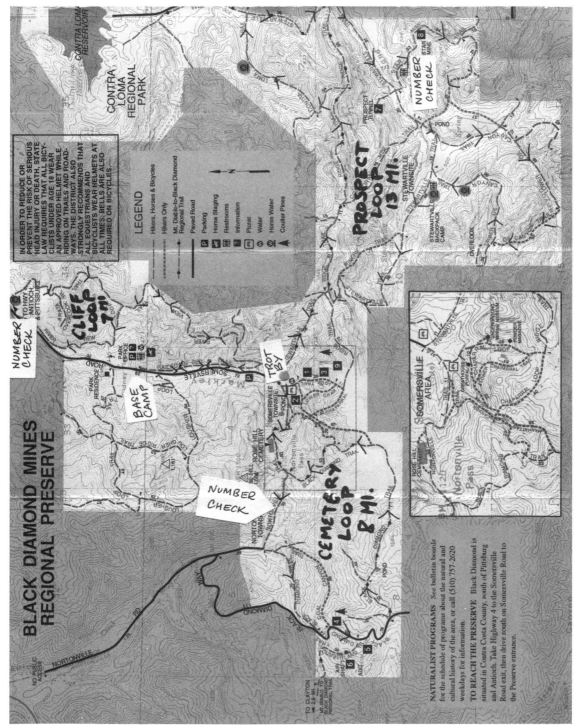

An example of a ride map, showing trails, water locations. (Note: On an actual ride map, the drawn trail is outlined in the same color as the ribbons used to mark the trail itself.)

accept their riders' control in an environment with this type of excessive stimulation. Needless to say, the start of the ride can be one of its most taxing and testing moments for both horse and rider.

Some rides have what is known as a *controlled start*. A little misleading, the name is given to a start where a point rider sets the pace for a specific distance— say one or more miles— before releasing participants to go at their own speed. It is often done when trail conditions make crowding dangerous or when the ride starts in the dark. While it is a little more organized than most shotgun starts, don't get the idea it is a walking-head-to-tail procession. It is not, and if the point rider's horse can trot faster than your horse, you'll find your horse trying to gallop to keep up.

A red ribbon tied into a strand of tail hair indicates a horse that kicks and is a warning to all riders not to approach too closely from behind. It is also a way of giving your horse a chance to get through the start without being run over or having its hind legs stepped on by a horse that is crowding from the rear.

ON THE TRAIL

Pacing

All horses have a speed at which they can travel for long periods of time over most types of country without tiring. Mileage studies have been done with wild horses that show they travel between 30 and 50 miles a day. It is up to you to keep your horse within its most efficient speed parameters as much as possible. The parameters may change as the horse becomes fitter and more experienced, but when you exceed that ideal pace, you will use up your horse too fast and could easily run out of horse before you run out of trail.

Two very successful riders, one from the East Coast and one from the West Coast show their understanding and use of pace, with the following comments. One says, "I can help an overridden horse recover and finish a ride in good shape if I slow the horse down to its own particular rhythm (or rate of speed)." The other says, "I never ride fast in order to top ten (which she achieves all the time), I just never go slow." Both have discovered the art of pacing their mounts.

No matter your starting position, try to settle your horse into its most efficient pace as soon as possible. Finding this pace at the start of a ride can be

Endurance riding probably won't cure cancer and won't earn you a Nobel prize, so take care of your horse and enjoy yourself! Photo: Pat Mitchell. ➤

more difficult than it sounds. Most horses want to keep up with or catch up to any horse they can see ahead. Once again, it's that instinctual "herd thing" at work. Now is when your training should help you control the horse and find his best pace. It also helps to have a riding buddy, especially if the horses know each other and are used to being ridden together. When this is the case, they will feel more comfortable in each other's company, especially if you are asking them to stay behind a group in front of you that is setting a faster pace than you want to ride or think is safe for your horse. Compromise, based on lots of training, will probably get you the best results on ride day. If your horse is fighting you tooth and nail, and acting like an idiot when you try to get him to settle, he will waste energy and may injure himself (if not you) as well. This being the case, rather than trying to keep your horse at the 8 mph trot you had in mind when you planned the ride, try to get your horse to meet you halfway and stay at 12 mph instead of the 15 mph he wants. If you can settle into that pace it will then be easier for you to gear down to the next level (10 mph). You will end up with the desired 8 mph pace quicker this way than if you fight the horse constantly or allow him to go wide open until he tires. Hanging on the bit is seldom a way to get control of your horse. Instead, bend his neck a little to one side or the other and hold him in this position until he slows. Use a verbal signal during training when you slow or stop the horse, and follow up the signal with some pretty significant repercussions if the horse fails to even try to do as you ask. If you do this often enough in training, your horse's obedience to your verbal signal will become a habit and *some* of it will stick with him in the heat of the ride, increasing your chances of being the one to regulate his gas pedal.

If you are riding a well-schooled horse with no control problems, great! You don't have too much to do but enjoy yourself and

- Ride your ride.

- Pay attention to footing, trail markers and your heart monitor.

- Decide what pace you want to ride the piece of trail on which you find yourself.

- Balance your horse in rough or deep footing.

- Watch for water.

- Be careful around other horses and riders on the trail, especially when you pass them or they pass you.

- Be aware of your body and mental state.

- Monitor your horse's emotional state.

- Smell the air.

- Oops, how did that vet check sneak up on you like that!

If you are going slow to get miles on a young horse, rehabilitate a horse with an old injury or "put a horse back together" that was overridden earlier in the ride, make sure you keep track of your cutoff times. AERC rules govern the time allowed to complete an event. Some ride managers are lenient about this rule, but others are not. It's very disheartening to cross the finish line late and be denied a completion.

The way you pace your horse on the trail will depend on the horse's level of fitness *on the day of the ride*, and where the horse is in its long-term training program (first ride, first year, second year, seasoned campaigner, etc.). While you may be able to take a horse and finish consistently in the top ten in its first year of competition, if you do, it is unlikely that horse will continue to do well for very long. Each ride should fit into the context of a long-range conditioning and maintenance plan. Failure to look ahead can lead you to overusing the horse on a short-term basis. Since a horse's system can sustain a fair amount of overwork before it begins to show stress by breaking down in various ways, cumulative strain can be difficult to assess. When your horse suddenly becomes mysteriously lame or fails to hold his condition like he did the previous year, stops eating and loses weight, stops having quick recoveries, etc., look back over your ride and/or training schedule for some answers. Ambition can be worse than pea soup fog in its capacity to reduce the ability to see clearly.

> If you are riding in hot weather, try to move along when your horse is in full sun and slow down when you find yourself in shade to take advantage of the shade's cooling effects.

Most horses have strengths and weaknesses when it comes to different trail topography. Some horses are strong uphill movers, while others seem to be able to fly downhill with almost no brakes on without pounding themselves or their riders unduly. Work during training to strengthen your horse's weak points, and use his strong points to your advantage during competition. If your horse struggles on steep hills, don't get sucked into trying to race into a vet check that is at the top of a steep climb. You may succeed in staying with a rider you eventually want to beat, but if your horse has had to use too much reserve doing it, its recovery will be poor, putting you behind in the overall picture. Better to slow down and ride the hill at the pace that is best for your horse—letting him recover quickly at the vet check—and use his downhill strength to overtake the rider once you are on the trail again. If you can't catch your competitors using that type of strategy, then the competitors have the better horses that day. If the competitors don't override their horses, they may continue to have the better horses for years to come. On the other hand, as you ride your horse within its limits, pushing the envelope a little each day in training, in a year or two your horse may finish first consistently. If your horse has it in him, you'll be able to get it out of him if you don't ask for too much too soon and use him up. Top competitors know how to wait for and recognize the right moment.

Trail Strategy

Strategy is part of the sport. Top riders definitely play the strategy game. I once listened to a rider tell how he polished off anyone who was dogging or pacing him—meaning laying just behind him on the trail, waiting for a race to the finish. He would, he said, wait for a spot where, unobserved, he could duck off the trail and out of sight of his pursuer. When the other rider could not see him anymore, she would push her horse, speeding up to try to catch him. He would then drop in behind her, keeping his horse at the pace that best suited it, and wait. Pretty soon, he said, his competitor had over-ridden her horse, was forced to slow down and drop back and he simply passed her smiling and continued down the trail to a win.

Racetrack folks have a word for the training strategy that takes advantage of the horse's natural instinct to want to stay with other horses. It's called *hooking.* If they want to encourage a horse who they feel isn't really trying his best, they take that horse out to train with another horse. The second horse's jockey has instructions to stay with the first horse for awhile, usually keeping her horse's nose at the shoulder of the first horse as they gallop around the track. Then the jockey of the second horse gradually begins to allow her horse to pull forward, perhaps even passing the first horse, but not pulling completely away. All the while this is happening, the first horse's jockey is urging his horse to try a little harder, telling his horse that he can really beat the horse next to him with just a little more effort. It is an effective technique.

The same technique, applied a little differently, is used in endurance riding. When ridden together, or in a group, one horse can pull others along. When the front horse tires, one of the horses that has been laying back in the pack moves to the front and takes the lead. The front horse will move back, but will still be pulled along with his buddies. This is a way to keep horses from experiencing the mental burnout that can happen when you are all alone on the trail. This technique can also be used against you. If you don't stay aware of your pacing, a competitor can pull your horse along and before you know it your horse is cooked, (all used up), while the competitor and his horse go merrily down the trail.

Endurance riding is an adventure. No one will ever win the Nobel Prize by getting to a finish line first, so it would be nice if everyone's conduct was appropriate to that thought. Unfortunately that philosophy is not consistent with human nature. But if you ride with the motto of AERC, "To finish is to win," as your first priority, you will find great joy and avoid the all-too-human trap of ego and the destruction it can cause.

There are still some strategies that you can fairly and rightfully use even when you are riding your own ride. Take the line with the best footing on any trail for your horse. Don't put your horse into ruts or rocks just to be polite. Give trail whenever it is requested by riders wishing to pass you, but do not put your horse or yourself into a dangerous spot to do so. Narrow trails and the challenges they present (including slower riders) are a part of the sport. Don't let riders push you into riding faster than you feel comfortable going by crowding you from behind; also, don't let them cut you off by diving to the inside on a sharp turn and rushing past. If they want to go around you, fine, let them take the outside track—unless you want to give them the space on the inside to pass. Where the safety of the animals are concerned, practice good sportsmanship and good horsemanship.

If you are at a watering hole and your horse has taken a few sips and along comes your competitor, you could let your horse rush off—which will probably unsettle your competitor's horse and keep it from drinking because it will want to go with you. But if you do that, you will reap what you sow in the community of endurance riders. Someday it will be your horse who desperately needs to drink and someone else will make it difficult for you. When at a watering hole or trough, if it is small, stay until your horse has had its fill, but then make room for anyone else on the scene, so that the rider's horse can access the water as well. If several horses are gathered at a watering spot, it is very bad manners to let your horse rub or dribble on the horse next to it, or splash in the water so other horses that are trying to get a drink are disturbed. If you are watering at a stream, pick the furthermost upstream position you can safely access. This way other horses can not muddy the water upstream from your horse, causing your horse to stop drinking. If you are in the upstream position and the water flow is limited, don't let your horse paw the stream bottom. That churns up silt that then fouls the water being drunk by the horses downstream from you.

When it comes to water, it is best to think of the horses and follow the Golden Rule of "Do unto others' horses as you would have them do unto yours." Don't try to play one-upmanship games with/at water.

Stay Focused

Staying conscious of where you are on the trail and understanding and using your trail map, as well as depending on the trail markers, is a good way to limit the number of times in your career you will find yourself off trail and lost. Hopefully, when this happens to you, you will pick it up quickly, backtrack to the last marker/ribbon you saw, and be able to find the correct trail by looking for tracks. Ribbons/trail markers have been known to be altered or removed, some by hikers, others by competitors. If you stay alert and use your trail map, you can usually catch a mistake quickly. If you should encounter a problem like a fallen tree or dead animal carcass that is blocking the trail, or an injured horse or rider, stop until you know if your help is needed or wanted. If necessary ride back to the last vet check or—once you have done all you can at the scene—ride quickly ahead to the next location where help might be available. Try to get specific information like whether the horse or rider are seriously hurt or endangered. If possible, wait for another rider to come along to stay with the injured rider while you go for help.

Some riders run parts of the trail with their horses, which is permitted by the rules. If you prefer to ride, you should consider tailing your horse up steep climbs. In tailing, you guide your horse by a line (usually some type of light cord attached to the bit) from behind, while holding on to its tail. This lets the horse pull you up hills rather than having to carry you up them. Practice tailing during training to accustom your horse to having you behind them. See Chapter 3, "Gymnastic Development of the Endurance Horse," for more detailed information on tailing.

Getting off and running downhill is easy if you are fit, especially if the trail is wide enough to allow you to run beside your horse. If that is the case, grab hold of a stirrup, the breast collar or (if you are tall enough and the horse is short), the pommel or handle of the saddle to stabilize yourself as you run. When you do this you can run much faster because you don't need to use a lot of muscles to hold your body back against gravity. Your grasp on the saddle or mane will keep you in balance.

Horses are very receptive and responsive to their rider's emotions and moods. If you let yourself become anxious, nervous, depressed or tired, you can expect your horse to change its behavior and attitude as well. Keep yourself "up" while you ride. If you are the type of person who needs company to enjoy yourself, then find some. If you feel yourself getting tired or anxious and are alone, talk out loud to your horse, or—better yet—sing! If this sounds silly to you, or a little over the edge, just ask any long-time, successful competitor whether or not they think their horse knows when they are tired or emotionally stressed. Their answer may surprise you.

Efficient Biomechanics

The balanced horse and rider have a great advantage on the trail because they can go faster, and/or longer over rough terrain (steep climbs and descents, rocks, slick footing, and so forth) with less damage to their body, legs, tendons and joints than the unbalanced horse. It is up to the rider to notice when her horse begins to tire and begins to carry more of its weight on the forehand. When this happens, some bridle contact will help keep your horse together a while longer, but if you override your horse's conditioning, you are increasing his risk of serious injury.

Change your posting diagonal every couple of miles to help your horse use both sides of its body evenly. When cantering or galloping for long periods of time, be sure to change your horse's leads regularly. You may need some practice at getting and recognizing the different leads, especially if you've never had any formal schooling in such things. Don't count on feeling comfortable to tell you which lead your horse is on or which diagonal you are posting to. If your horse is weak and/or stiff on one side he won't want to take that lead or have you post on his weak diagonal. If you do, his gait may feel rough, causing you to unconsciously change back in an attempt to feel more comfortable. Most horses, unless they have been thoroughly schooled and balanced, will favor one lead over another. Your horse will choose his favorite every time if you let *him* be the one to decide.

Hill Work

Keep in mind if your horse accelerates downhill, he will have to use a lot more energy to stop himself at the bottom. Slamming on the brakes at the bottom of a hill causes jarring to the joints and tendons. If the hill is steep and followed by another uphill section of trail (a roller-coaster type of trail), your horse could try to leave out the last stride into the very lowest point of the trail, taking a small hop to land ascending the hill in front of him. Although he does this so that his momentum will make climbing the next hill easier, hitting the uphill grade with all that downhill force is a good way to strain or tear something in his front legs. Letting the horse release his brakes just before the bottom of the hill so that his momentum carries him partway up the next hill is a good strategy to save energy *only* if the angle of rolling terrain is gentle with long soft curves or some flat ground between hills. If your horse is fit and in good condition, you can let him go straight down a hill. If he is tired, allow him to zigzag from side to side. The horse who goes straight down must use both hind legs and all the large muscles of his hindquarters to resist gravity with every stride. When the horse is allowed to walk back and forth across the trail, one leg rests while the other leg does most of the work. This is better for the tired horse.

Vet Checks

There is no question, the rider who knows the trail has a distinct advantage. Whether you preride it in training or simply compete at the same rides year after year, knowing where the tough spots are and where you can make time with your horse gives you an advantage. The other benefit to be had by knowing the trail is knowing where you are in relation to your vet checks. This includes knowing in advance what type of topography you will hit before the check. Top riders plan their pace (as much as they can), to arrive at the various vet checks along the trail with their horses able to recover in a few minutes. This may mean backing off the pace when they know they are about to come into a check. Some rides make this easy by alerting riders with markings on the trail telling them the distance to the check. If you are riding your horse well within his capacity, say around 120 beats per minute (bpm) on the heart-rate monitor—and the last mile isn't all up hill—you can maintain your pace right into the check. If you are running at a higher rate, you will need to know how fast your horse recovers in order to keep going right up to the check without losing time waiting for the heart rate to drop to criteria level before you can have your hold time start. When you arrive at your vet check your crew goes to work, helping get the horse's pulse and respiration down, icing its legs or keeping the muscles warm, massaging the horse, working the accupressure points on the ear for quicker recovery, making sure the horse has water to drink and offering it anything it will eat, removing the saddle (if that is required/desired), and allowing the horse to urinate. Sometimes the crew might even form a human ring around the horse so spectators don't crowd too close, preventing the horse from relaxing and eating.

There are two basic types of vet checks that include holds, the *straight hold* and the *gate to a hold*. The gate to a hold check rewards the horse that recovers fast or the rider who is riding her horse well within its parameters, because the official hold clock is not started until the horse meets the pulse and respiration criteria for the stop. A horse and rider could arrive ten minutes ahead of the next rider, but go out on the trail ten minutes after the second rider, if the first rider's horse takes 20 minutes to recover to the criteria, while the second rider's horse comes down within a minute or two. At top-level competitions such as the National Championships and the World Championships, medals are won and lost in the vet checks.

Recovery criteria is usually set somewhere between 60 and 68 bpm, and a horse that is not being overridden should be able to reach this figure within 10 minutes of arrival.

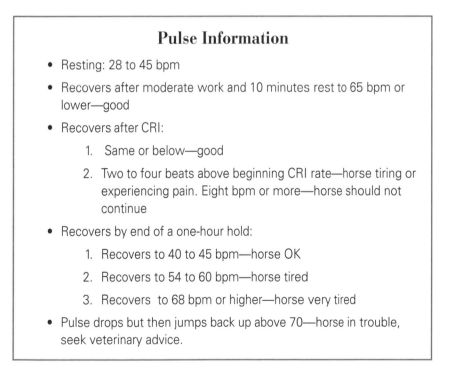

Pulse Information

- Resting: 28 to 45 bpm
- Recovers after moderate work and 10 minutes rest to 65 bpm or lower—good
- Recovers after CRI:
    1. Same or below—good
    2. Two to four beats above beginning CRI rate—horse tiring or experiencing pain. Eight bpm or more—horse should not continue
- Recovers by end of a one-hour hold:
    1. Recovers to 40 to 45 bpm—horse OK
    2. Recovers to 54 to 60 bpm—horse tired
    3. Recovers to 68 bpm or higher—horse very tired
- Pulse drops but then jumps back up above 70—horse in trouble, seek veterinary advice.

When you arrive at the vet check, you will either get a time card or the in-timer will mark your arrival time on your vet card. When your horse meets the recovery criteria for the hold, your official hold time will start/be recorded by the P & R (pulse and respiration) person, and your "out" time (the time you are released to go back on the trail) will also be noted. You, or your crew, must present your horse to the vet sometime during that hold period. Most riders like to present right away, while the horse's muscles are still warmed up and loose from its work on the trail. Generally speaking, this is a good idea, but you need to take a moment to look at your horse when you come in to determine if a little TLC by your crew would make the horse present better. If the hold time allows, getting your horse to drink and/or urinate before presenting to the vet may help your overall vet score.

Keep track of your time card if it is separate from your vet card, because you will need it to give/show to the out-timer to be officially released from the stop. If the stop is a straight-timed hold, you are simply timed in and given an out time corresponding to the stated hold time of the stop. For example, if the hold time is one half hour, and your arrival time is 11:21 A.M., your departure time will be 11:51 A.M.

When vets examine a horse during a vet check they look at all the metabolic factors to see how the horse is doing. They also ask the rider questions about the horse. "How is your horse doing? Is it drinking, and eating? Has it urinated?" Your answers are an important part of the information the vets need to do their job of protecting the horse during the ride. You may be disappointed if you get pulled, but you'd feel a whole lot worse if your horse died on the trail, and it *has* happened. It is important for you to know what's normal and note any changes. You know your horse better than the vet. A small change that would not ordinarily concern a vet might be a major warning sign for your horse. Doing your part is not just staying on and steering.

You will be asked to trot the horse as a part of the veterinarian exam, so the vet can watch for any sign of lameness or altered gait. A horse that exhibits a lame step every once in a while when trotted out (grade one lame) may be allowed to continue, if the vet can see that the soreness is not structural but is coming from a cut, abrasion or bruise. If the horse's discomfort level increases by the next check, the horse and rider will be pulled.

Respiration is not usually a reason to hold a horse, but panting can indicate overheating. If your horse pants, be prepared to spend extra time cooling it down before presenting it to the vet. Any signs of metabolic distress, such as those in the following list, are reason to pull the horse/rider team:

A rider trotting her horse for the vet. ➤

- A long capillary refill time

- A prolonged tenting with the skin pinch

- A sustained high heart rate or breathing pattern

- A CRI that shows a substantial increase in pulse rate after the trot out

- No gut sounds

- Dark or coffee-colored urine

Your vet card has spaces for the vet to indicate his or her findings—usually by means of an alphabetical grade, such as A (good), B (fair), C (acceptable but borderline) and D (poor). Look the grade over after the check. If you have any questions, or have a less than optimum score, consult the vet for more information and his or her opinion about how the score should affect your riding and pacing plans on the next leg of the ride.

After you and your crew have gotten your horse through the vet check, take any extra time you have left and continue to work on the horse to increase its comfort level, help it cool, improve its mental state and—oh, yes—rest! If there is green grass available and the horse doesn't prefer something else, take off the bridle and let them munch all they want, since it has a high water content. If the weather is hot, and a stream is available, letting your horse stand in it up to its knees for about ten minutes is a good way of cooling its feet and legs. Do not do this with a tired horse, or at night when the horse might chill easily. If your crew is good, let them do their job and spend some time taking care of yourself: eat, drink, clean up (if time permits) and rest (sit down and take some deep breaths). Have someone massage your back, neck, shoulders and the calves of your legs. Take your shoes off and change your socks if they are damp. With your shoes off, stretch out your toes and wiggle them, then put them in a basin of cool water if it is a hot day and place a cold wet rag over your head and face for a couple of minutes. Drink, drink, drink! Anything you can do to refresh yourself physically and mentally will benefit your horse. As time approaches to leave the check, get all your gear back on your horse, and do a last minute check of things like water bottles, glow bars, trail snacks, and extra clothing if you're riding into dusk and the temperature might drop. It is easy to chill when you are tired. Give your horse his electrolytes before putting his bridle back on.

> Giving electrolytes is an accepted practice today in the sport of endurance riding, but we are still learning about what the long-distance equine athlete needs to keep it healthy and make its job easier. There is a link between the salts in electrolytes and the part of the horse's brain that signals thirst. If electrolytes become depleted too quickly, a circuit is broken and the horse may not know it needs to drink; therefore, it won't. If the horse is not drinking, some riders will not give electrolytes, while others will administer an additional amount. Since an electrolyte imbalance in the horse can result in poor recovery, fast or irregular heart rate, and extreme fatigue, it is essential to know your horse. Experiment with electrolyte dosages during training to learn what works best for him, then take the necessary precautions during a ride to see the horse has what its system needs, even if it means stopping on the trail rather than waiting until a vet check to administer additional electrolytes.

The further along in a ride you progress, the more reluctant your horse may be to leave the stop, especially if you are riding several repetitions on the same loop or if your horse's buddy with whom you've been riding the past 35 miles got pulled at the check. A young horse or a horse new to the sport, not knowing how far it is expected to travel before being allowed to quit, may be reluctant to continue. A horse can suffer from mental depression the first time it is asked to move to a longer distance. It will be up to you to decide if your horse has reached his limits, either in distance or speed, and back off, or is mentally depressed. If the latter is the case, find another rider to buddy with. Company will help improve your horse's mental state. It is not always an easy call, so listen to your gut instincts and consider the horse's recovery criteria. If necessary, delay your departure from the check to hook up with another horse and rider.

THE FINISH LINE

When you cross the finish line you will feel elated. Most riders hug their horse, their husband (or wife) and their crew, not always in that order. Some cry, some collapse, some are speechless and others you can't shut up. Your crew will help you cool the horse down, making sure its pulse and respiration are down to the final required numbers before returning to the recheck. In order to officially complete a ride, your horse must pass a final vet check, usually within one hour of finishing. Take your time and do all the things you've been doing all day to help keep your horse in good shape. If the weather is hot, you will need to cool the horse. If it is night time you will need to keep him from chilling and becoming stiff. Remember your horse is tired. Think logically and use your common sense. You want him to drink, but too much cold water can keep his pulse up as his body pulls energy from its depleted stores to warm the cold water in his belly. You want him to eat, but his digestive system doesn't have access to the energy or blood supply to digest a large quantity of grain, so letting him bolt large amounts of grain after coming in may result in colic. Massage is good at this point, and unless it is hot, put a cooler over his tired muscles. Sponge his legs, chest, belly, head and neck. Every 20 minutes or so, walk him around slowly for five minutes before letting him stand again. Offer him things he likes to eat, like carrots and apples. Put some molasses and salt in a warm bran mash and offer him that to eat. Many riders ice their horse's legs. If you do not do this, at least use some rubbing alcohol and rub his legs vigorously until they are dry. After the recheck, brush his coat and spend some time scratching the itchy places. If there is a good sandy place take him there and let him roll to scratch his own back. Be sure your horse is content and appears happy and settled before going to the banquet. If you have any doubts, have one of your crew stay with him, or take him to a vet.

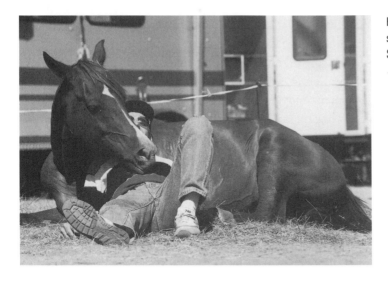

Horse and crew catch a little shuteye. Photo: Genie Stewart-Spears.

◄

The awards banquet is where finishing awards are given out, as well as awards such as First Place, Best Condition and Top Ten. Some rides also give weight division awards, breed awards, and junior division awards. One California ride offers a Pissin' 'n' Moanin' award, and occasionally a ride honors the last rider to finish with a "tail-end" award. A meal with friends and crew discussing the challenges and delights of the days trail is a great closure. If you won, tired or not, you'll feel like celebrating. If luck or circumstances turned against you and you were pulled, there will be other riders who have had a similar experience. Sharing can bring wisdom and an understanding silence can be a powerful place of healing. The awards banquet is a good place to thank the ride management and volunteers for their efforts. Without them this sport wouldn't exist and nobody gets rich from running a ride. The appreciation of the riders goes a long way toward making it worth doing again next year. If the ride had sponsors, a note to them thanking them for their support is a sure way to keep future awards coming. If the ride was held on public land, a state or national park, a note to the park service supervisor would be a major kudo for the sport. It all takes time but you can look at it as payback for the privilege of the adventure. Not many people get to visit with God in his own house.

Best Condition Judging

The Best Condition award is considered by some riders to be the crowning achievement in endurance riding. It is determined by a three-part procedure based on riding time, weight carried and a veterinary score (postride examination). The postride BC judging takes place sometime after the first ten competitors have crossed the finish line (management usually gives the time and place of the BC judging at the rider briefing). If you finish in the top ten, you must weigh-in immediately after dismounting, before you leave the finish line area. Your weight includes you, your tack, and any equipment, such as water bottles, Easy Boots, etc., that is attached to your saddle and accompanied you through the ride.

Needless to say you want to present the horse in top shape, looking his or her best. While the endurance field is not a show ring, it does the sport credit if the top ten horses show the efforts of their riders and crews when they are presented. Horses should not be shown for BC with sweat marks, looking dirty, tired and depressed. If you finished in the top ten your horse gave a good effort. If that effort cost more than you had intended, you may wish to withdraw from the BC judging and wait until another ride when you can present your horse showing outstanding recovery and condition. Crews go all out to prepare their horses for the BC judging, sometimes staying up all night at 100-mile events like the Tevis (BC at Tevis is judged on the morning following the ride) to massage, walk, ice and work on their horses. If your horse is honored with the award, it is an unforgettable moment, whether it happens at a local 50-mile race or the Race Of Champions.

If you are campaigning for regional or national points, placing first in your weight division, placing in the top ten and/or receiving the best condition award at a ride, gives you additional points.

AERC has guidelines for the veterinarians judging BC. The veterinary portion of the score is defined as "the horse, at the time of the Best Condition examination, that is in the best condition and deemed most fit to continue." The actual award is modified from the veterinary-defined portion to allow for finish time and weight factors.

The finishing time factor is evaluated by entering the riding time (excluding fixed hold times) of all eligible riders on the time portion of the BC score sheet. The first-to-finish rider gets 200 points, and all other riders get one point less per minute they are behind the first-to-finish rider. The weight factor is reached by assigning a value of 100 points to the heaviest weight rider to finish in the top ten and subtracting 1/2 point per pound for all other eligible riders.

AERC guidelines allow the ride vet to elect not to award a best condition "if none of the horses evaluated are worthy in the opinion of the veterinary

AMERICAN ENDURANCE RIDE CONFERENCE

ADMINISTRATIVE OFFICE:
701 HIGH STREET, SUITE 203 • AUBURN, CA 95603
916-823-2260

RIDER NO. _____

BEST CONDITION EVALUATION

RIDE NAME _____ REGION _____ DISTANCE _____ RIDE DATE _____

RIDER'S NAME _____ **RIDER'S WT _____ FINISH PLACE _____

RIDER'S FINISH TIME _____ (hrs) _____ (min) HORSE'S NAME _____

***The Rider's finishing weight is determined at the conclusion of
the ride with tack and the same clothes worn during the ride.*

A. VETERINARY SCORE SHEET   MAXIMUM SCORE 500 POINTS

STANDING EVALUATION

Recovery:
Base upon ability to demonstrate recovery e.g. the Cardiac Recovery index-Recommend use the CRI taken 10 or 15 minutes post finish time. Base the respiratory aspects on quality of respiration as determined visually and by auscultation

SCORE 1-10 _____

Hydration Factors:
Use all the metabolic parameters that indicate the stae of hydration, i.e.: Skin Tenting, Mucous Membranes, Capilary Refill Time, Jugular Refill Time and Gut Sounds

SCORE 1-10 _____
RANGE

Lesions Producing Pain and Discomfort:
Major concerns are Back Pin and pain/swelling in Joints, Tendon, and Ligaments that may be indicative of potentially serious pathology. Also consider Girth, Saddle, and other Tack Induced Lesions and all Wounds. Note: do all but cursory palpatation after the movement phase

SCORE 1-10 _____

MOVEMENT EVALUATION

Soundness:
*Note: Not eligible for consideration for B.C. if there is a pathologial gait aberation greater than grade II.
Consider: Regularity of gait and movement*

SCORE 1-10 _____
RANGE

Quality of Movement:
Consider: Attitude, Coordination and Impulsion (deterioration exhibited as a reluctance or refusal to trot, stumbling, leg weariness, muscle fatigue and stiffness)

SCORE 1-10 _____

SUBTOTAL _____

TOTAL VETERINARY SCORE = SUBTOTAL X 10 _____

Parts B and C to be completed by Ride Management ONLY (To be done after veterinary completion of Part A)

B. TIME FACTOR   MAXIMUM 200 POINTS (Awarded to Fastest Rider)

Riding Time of THIS rider	_____	*(Value one point per minute)*
Riding Time of Winner	_____	MAXIMUM _____ 200
Difference:	_____	LESS DIFFERENCE (-) _____
(calculate time in munutes - exclude hold times)		TOTAL TIME SCORE _____

C. WEIGHT FACTOR   MAXIMUM 100 POINTS (Awarded to the Heaviest Rider)

Weight of Heaviest Rider	_____	*(Value one/half point per pound)*
Weight of THIS Rider	_____	MAXIMUM _____ 100
Difference ÷ 2	_____	LESS DIFFERENCE ÷ 2 (-) _____
		TOTAL WEIGHT SCORE _____

TOTAL SCORE = A + B + C = _____

RIDE MANAGER _____ HEAD VETERINARIAN _____

*This score sheet must accompany AERC Ride Results for Winner to be eligible for Regional and National Awards.
Mail original copy to AERC with Ride Results, second copy to Ride Manager, Third copy to rider.*

AERC B.C. FORM: 8-95.1

The form provided by the AERC and used by ride managers and vets for the Best Condition Horse Award evaluation.

examining committee because of low scores." To insure that the horses have a chance to show at their best after putting forth a top-ten effort in a race, vets are instructed by AERC guidelines to do the movement (trot out) phase of the BC exam before any palpation/flexion tests are done on the horses, and to "avoid excessive pressure on all flexion tests." Impulsion is rewarded in the BC judging, but defined as "the horse's willingness to move forward" (the rules discourage hazing, cautioning judges to differentiate between "hype" and "a true state of ability to continue").

In cases of a tie, the best veterinary score (without factoring in either ride time or rider weight) will break the tie.

AFTER THE RIDE

If you rode to finish, your horse is looking fresh and frisky and you have only a few hours to trailer home, there is not much concern beyond what you would ordinarily do to insure comfort and safety with your horse in any hauling situation. If, however, your horse was stressed by his ride effort, you need to consider delaying your departure for home until the animal has recovered, has eaten, drunk and completed other normal bodily functions at least several times. Most endurance rides are held on a Saturday, so if necessary you can camp an additional night to allow your horse extra recovery time. If your trailer-time home is eight hours or more, stop more frequently than you did on the way to the ride, allowing the horse to drink and rest. If the weather is cold, blanket your horse, but when you stop open the trailer windows/feed doors to circulate fresh air. Check also to be sure the air in the trailer is not becoming too humid. This can happen in aluminum trailers that are tightly sealed, especially if you have two or three horses aboard. Every four hours, stop and un-load the horse and walk him around a bit. During that time you can observe him closely for signs that might indicate he is experiencing stress or is in trouble. If the weather is hot, provide as much ventilation as possible in the trailer. Park in the shade when you stop—or better yet, try to get most of your roadtime done in the cooler hours of the early morning, evening or at night.

I like to wrap my horse's legs after a ride, giving support and warmth for at least 24 hours.

When wrapping a leg for support, apply a cotton quilt to the tendon area before beginning to bandage.

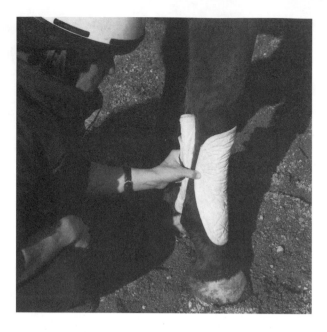

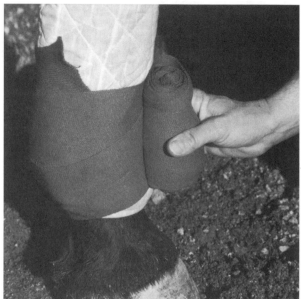

Start the leg bandage just above the fetlock joint and wrap down under the joint before continuing to bring the wrap up the leg. ➤

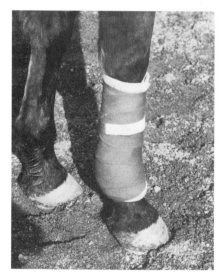

A leg showing a good bandaging job, smooth and snug with no wrinkles.

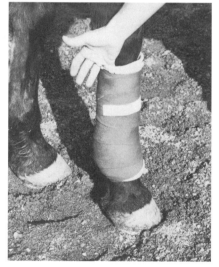

Check to see that the bandage is not too tight by inserting your little finger in the space between the cannon bone and the tendon after wrapping the leg. The wrap should feel snug but should not constrict the circulation in your finger.

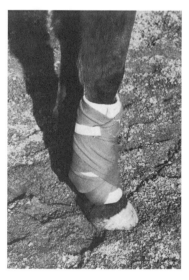

A poor leg-bandaging job. If left on for a long trailer trip or overnight, this wrap could cause tendon problems from uneven pressure.

To do this, you need some cotton quilts and the type of wrap called "track" or "knit" wraps, not flannel or polo wraps. Apply the quilts between the knee and ankle of the horse. Start by placing the edge of the quilt in the groove between the cannon bone and the tendon, then wrap it around the cannon smoothly, making sure it is snug without being tight, twisted, or wrinkled. Start the knit bandage at about three-fingers height above the fetlock joint, making a couple of turns around the leg toward the ground, then bringing the wrap diagonally down under the horse's fetlock and back up again, proceeding to wrap back up the cannon from there. This type of application will support tired tendons. Continue to wrap up snugly under the knee in order to support the check ligament.

Bandaging for a support wrap. ➤

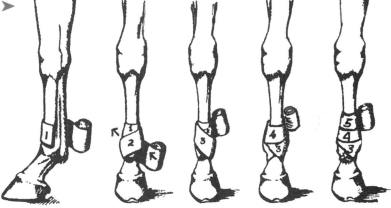

If you are inexperienced at wrapping a leg, it is a good idea to seek some instruction and supervision during your first few attempts. Wrapping a leg well takes practice. Bandaging or wrapping legs can support tired tendons, reduce filling and protect the leg during trailering; it can also do serious damage if the bandage is applied in a sloppy manner, becomes twisted and tightens unevenly, or if it is left on too long.

Remove the wraps the next morning to check your horse's legs. If your horse's tendons are hot, apply a poultice and rewrap, changing the poultice and wraps daily, until all the heat is out of the leg(s). Continue to rub the legs with a liniment and wrap them for several more days. Apply liniment and rub the legs, until your horse's legs are once again tight.

Bandaging Rules

1. Never draw one part of the bandage tighter than any other part.
2. Never draw the Velcro or string tighter than any other part of the wrap.
3. Never bandage so tightly that circulation is restricted.
4. Check the evenness of pressure by inserting the little finger of your hand in the tendon groove at both the top and bottom of the bandage when you have finished wrapping the leg.

It is not uncommon for some horse's legs to stock up after working. Many endurance horses are kept in pastures or large paddocks and so have the advantage of moving around more than their cousins, the show horses. This movement tends to keep stocking to a minimum. You can tell the difference between a stocked leg and a leg swollen from strain by the presence or absence of heat (stocked legs are not usually hot to the touch), and also by pressing your finger or thumb into the swollen area of the leg. If a hollow forms under pressure and stays after you remove your finger, the leg is stocked up (has an accumulation of fluid in the tissues). Light exercise, rubbing and bandaging for a day or two are what is called for if this occurs. If the swelling feels hot to the touch, the horse shows discomfort upon being moved or worked, or displays soreness upon palpation of the leg, call your vet for advice.

Let your horse have some time off after a ride, followed by light work. If the ride was only 25 miles, a couple of days will do. If the ride is a 50 miler, I let my horses have a week off following the ride. After a 100, my horses get to vacation for two weeks.

Do not confine your horse to a stall during this rest period. Allow him to roam about a pasture if possible. Restrict or eliminate concentrates during the rest period. I like to take my horses off all grain if they are not actively training, giving them only a handful of rice bran with their vitamins each day as a treat until I put them back to work again. Failing to do this is the primary cause of horses tying up when put back to work. Reducing or withholding grain during long trailering trips is also advised for the same reason. When withholding grain, I feed my horses all the hay they want to eat, unless they have access to quality pasture in abundance.

APPENDICES

THE PEOPLE YOU MEET

Valerie Kanavy

Age: 50

Mileage: 8,000+

Profession: Wife, mother and endurance rider

Special Achievements:

Danielle and Valerie Kanavy receiving the gold and silver medal at the 1996 World Endurance Championships. Photo: Genie Stewart-Spears.

- World Endurance Champion 1994

- AERC National 100 Mile Champion 1994

- IAHA National Endurance Champion and ROC winner 1995

- Individual and Team Bronze Medal, 1995 North American Championships

- Individual Silver Medalist, World Endurance Championships 1996

Why endurance?

"I like the challenge and the partnership with the horse. I enjoy taking a horse from the beginning and creating a top-caliber athlete. Endurance gives a purpose to my riding and training."

Your favorite horse?

"All of my horses are favorites with me and I admire each one for different reasons. Currently Pieraz (known as 'Cash') has been the most famous and successful. I bought him as a green-broke Arabian gelding for experienced rider only. With a record of nearly thirty 100-mile events, all in the top ten, we often joke that riding Cash is like purchasing a ticket to finish. He is lazy at the beginning of a ride, gathering interest and becoming determined to win toward the finish. Indeed, his 'don't work any harder than necessary' attitude, combined with the many years of careful, consistent, progressive training has turned this backyard horse into a formidable competitor and twice winner of the World Championship title in endurance."

Danielle Kanavy

Age: 25
Mileage: 3,310
Profession: Nursing
Special Achievements:

- Winning a National Championship at age 10
- Being the only Junior to ever win the Old Dominion Ride (age 15)
- Winning two Gold Medals at the World Endurance Championships in Kentucky in 1996

Why endurance?

"I like the sport because it is not subjective. I enjoy the challenge and I love training the horses and riding them to keep them fit. I also enjoy nature and getting to see the countryside."

Your favorite horse?

"All my horses are my favorite. I spent a lot of time with Sonny, earning his trust, so he is the one I remember the most. When he was killed in a freak accident in Wyoming in 1995, it devastated me. I still feel his loss. Now I'm riding his brother, Fire, and he is my favorite because he forces me to think and work when I ride."

Melissa Crain

Age: 46
AERC Mileage: 4,000
Profession: Homemaker and mother
Special achievements:

Member USET endurance squad 1994 World Equestrian Games. Photo: Genie Stewart-Spears.

- Third in Race of Champions 1992

- Winning Race Of Champions 1993

- AERC Lightweight National Champion 1994

- Member of the USET in World Equestrian Games in Holland, completing the ride

- Member of Central Time Zone team at North American Championships 1995, finished sixth

- The World Endurance Championships in Kansas 1996, finished ninth

Why endurance?

"If you're a horsewoman and have some horse sense, endurance riding is something you can be competitive in and do well when you're older. It's also the most inexpensive horse sport I've found."

Your favorite horse?

"My favorite horse is Whoa Jack. He is the sweetest, kindest Arabian that ever was. He always gives a hundred percent and knows just what to do. Jack has taught me so much and I'm still learning. He is seventeen now and still sound, enthusiastic and going strong. My favorite pit crew is my husband Tommy. I couldn't do a 100 without his support. I feel fortunate to have these two special friends in my life."

Mathew P. Mackay-Smith, D.V.M.

Age: 65
AERC Mileage: Over 5,000
Profession: Veterinarian and journalist
Special achievements:

Winner Tevis and Old Dominion 1995.
Photo: Genie Stewart-Spears.

- Placing fifth in the Tevis on my first-ever endurance ride

- Winning the Old Dominion 100 on five different horses

- Winning both the Old Dominion and the Tevis on the same horse in 1995

- Pulling out of a ride because I was there for the wrong reasons

- Being named to the AERC Hall of Fame

Why endurance?

"To better understand and appreciate horses in a natural setting and use. To see new country and meet like-minded people."

Your favorite horse?

"The horse that stands out for me from all the horses I've competed over my years in this sport is Gwali Ibn Oran. His seller told me, 'He'll give you a lot but he won't take much.' Wali, as we called him, taught me to speak and understand 'horse.' He taught me more of the truth about horses than all the others I have known, combined. He was a constant trial, mentally and physically, because his belief in himself was so much larger than any reality of flesh and blood. He saw mountains as flat, boulder fields as paved; no lion had such heart. Only he and I can know the transcendent moments we had. His kind will not pass my way again."

Maryben Stover

Age: 55
AERC Mileage: 7,485
Profession: Legal secretary
Special achievements:

West Region Heavyweight Champion
1987. Photo: Pat Mitchell.

- My first 100-mile ride when World Champion
  Becky Hart crewed for me!

- Being West Region Heavyweight Champion
  in 1987

- Having Q-Ball and Scarlett (my mule) reach
  2,000 miles

- Sponsoring juniors on rides and getting to
  watch them grow into wonderful people

- Sponsoring juniors Larrissa Voight, Heather Bergantz and Julie
  Caprino, all of whom have won the AERC National Junior
  Championship

Why endurance?

"I think endurance is the most fun and the most rewarding
experience you can have with your horse (or mule). I have met all
my closest friends through endurance and owning horses. You
can be rich or poor, it doesn't matter. With endurance you get to
ride your horse in places that most people don't even get to see,
and going to a ride is like a minivacation. You forget about
everyday problems."

Your favorite horse?

"My mule Scarlett is huge and intimidating when you first see
her up close, but she is very timid, extremely gentle and smooth
to ride. Somewhere during our first 50, we made a deal, Scarlett
picks the pace and I get to steer; so far its worked out pretty well,
we're getting close to 3,000 miles.

My heros are Julie Suhr, Becky Hart and the Waltenspiels, and I miss the good people and horses who are now gone, like Smokey and Bandit, John Plaggmier, Virl Norton, Don Evenson, Mae Schlaegal and Lad. Virl Norton introduced me to mules in 1975. He told me he thought he could win the Great American Horse Race with his mules Lord Fauntleroy and Lady Eloise and he did!"

Janet Canfield

Age: 53 "years young"
Mileage: 2,105
Profession: Secretary
Special achievements:

- Getting through my first 50

- Getting through my first 100

- My first top-ten finish

- Placing 22nd at the Race of Champions in 1996

Fifty-three years young. Photo: Joyce Brown.

Why Endurance?

"I find endurance riding challenging, relaxing, exhilarating, peaceful, enjoyable and frustrating in turns, but the main reasons I ride are the enjoyment of the equine and human companionship, the feeling of accomplishment and the beautiful country."

Your favorite horse?

"God's second greatest gift to womankind surely was the horse. During the past five years my horse, Tequila's Shadow, an Appaloosa mare, now fourteen, and I have entered 41 endurance rides, finishing 40. We started trail riding to condition *me*, with no thought of competing. As my confidence grew, I entered my first ride and promptly became hooked (I think the sport should come with a warning label about being addictive). I am grateful to be part of a sport where people can compete, laugh, care and have companionship with one another as well as with their equine partners. The next goal for Shadow and me is the Tevis."

Jan Worthington

Age: 56
Mileage: 13,500
Profession: Farmer
Special Achievements:

- My very first ROC when I finished fifth and couldn't believe it!

- Being selected for the U.S. squad for the World Championships in both 1987 and 1996.

USET squad 1996 World Championships. Photo: Genie Stewart-Spears.

Why endurance?

"To test myself and my horses over the course for that day. To see if my conditioning is on target. To meet the neat people from all over the world."

Your favorite horse?

"My partner Grace Ramsey bought L. M. Mastermind as a two-year-old. I was mad at her for buying a horse we couldn't ride for two more years. When we started him as a four-year-old on 25-mile competitive rides, he was so easy going we let a lot of different people ride him. When he turned seven, he showed some real promise and I leased him for the North American in Calgary, Canada, where he finished eleventh! That was when I decided he would be my horse and we would aim for being selected to represent the U.S. at the World Championships. I love him for his laid-back attitude. He never gets upset, no matter how "hyper" *I* get. His farrier says he never wears his shoes because he hits the ground so lightly with his feet."

Maggie Price

Age: 64

Mileage: 6,000+

Profession: Endurance rider & horse breeder

Special achievements:

- Placing in the top ten eight times out of ten at the ROC

- Top Ten at the Tevis several times

- Won Swanton Pacific in 1984

- Bronze Medal on the US team in Spain in 1992

- AERC Hall of Fame

Bronze Medal 1992 World Championships in Spain.

Why Endurance?

"My favorite activity on horseback is to find a hole in the woods and follow the path. Even though I was born too late to explore with Lewis and Clark, I find exploring the greatest fun. Add the thrill of competing to that and you have my favorite sport—endurance riding!"

Your favorite horse?

"Ramegwa Kanavyann ('Annie' to her friends) was a little (850 pounds) Arab mare I rode in the World Championships in Spain in 1992. We finished the ride in ten hours and won the Bronze Medal. She really enjoyed trotting through the thickest woods and galloping down the roads. She was laid-back around camp, hated the trot-outs at vet checks (thought they were an imposition) and could be a maniac if she chose to be. She made me learn more than any horse I'd ever had and would frequently review me if she thought I'd forgotten. But in Spain she decided she was cut out to be a movie star. Nothing bothered her, not the cheering, parades or the airplane trip. Her attitude was totally 'Throw more roses!'

I'm still throwing roses at her. This summer she gave me her first foal, a gorgeous filly by Desparado."

Judy Van Meter

Age: 57

Mileage: 5,795

Profession: Retired mother of five, grandmother of seven.

Special achievements:

- I've ridden the same horse on the Old Dominion six consecutive years and placed in the top ten twice

- I always ride my horse at a "completion" pace, never race, and have won the AERC Northeast Lightweight Division title three times

Northeast Region Lightweight Champion. Photo: Genie Stewart-Spears.

Why endurance?

"For the adventure and fun. I love horses and riding and love to ride really long rides that go someplace."

Your favorite horse?

"My favorite horse is a Saddlebred-Arab cross called Beau Prince ('Thunder'). He was sold in a 'killer' sale in California. He worked his way East through a series of owners, all of whom rejected him eventually because of his misbehavior or soundness problems, until he ended up with me. It took me nine years of tender loving care to completely uncover his kind, wonderful temperament. He retired sound at eighteen with over 2,000 miles.

This sport has given me some of the best days of my life. My husband Norman is a great crew. My daughter Jeanne and my granddaughter Barbara rode with me on the Bucks County ride in Pennsylvania. It was great to have three generations riding together. Endurance is probably the only sport in the world where a grandmother can ride alongside her daughters and granddaughters and place ahead of them!"

Heather Bergantz

Age: 19

Mileage: 5,500

Profession: Work at a day care school

Special achievements:

- Winning the 1993 Junior National AERC Championship

- Riding R. O. Grand Sultan (World Champion Horse) in some rides

- Getting a straight 10 vet score on my horse Tyler at his first 100-miler

- Finishing the Tevis 20th on Tyler on our first try

National Champion Junior Rider 1993.

Why endurance?

"I like to compete. Endurance will let you compete but at the same time you can see your friends and hang out in camp. It's really just a big social event with a race at the end."

Your favorite horse?

"My horse Tyler is always telling me that we just aren't going fast enough. When I bought him he only had three gaits—walk, jog and run—and the jog was just to get to the run. When I was trying him out, I took him on the Fort Churchill 100 to see if he could do it. He ended up losing by a nose, and finishing in 10 hours; but the next day he got straight tens at the Best Condition judging. At the Sonoma 50, I wanted to be about 20th, but Tyler had other plans. He finished third and I bought him. He's done all three championship rides, and with Becky Hart sponsoring us at the final ride, we did the 100 under 9 hours and he looked great. After a serious injury in '94, Tyler came back in '96 to compete and win for me again. He's the greatest."

Glen Cox and Nancy Cox

Ages: 48; 47

Mileage: 3,925; 5,330

Professions: Diesel mechanic; tax consultant

Special Achievements: Glen

- Won my horse at the Chief Paulina 50

- Completed ROC 27th

- Won the Flying M 75-miler and BC in my first year of competition

Special Achievements: Nancy

- 1,000 miles on my first horse, Rakar

- 3,000 miles on my second horse, Mister Shadrach

- Winning the Paulina 100-milers with the help of my crew

- Completing ROC in Utah

- Taking a friend through her first 50

Five thousand miles on two horses since 1973. Photo: Brown's Photography.

"Won my horse at the Chief Paulina 50." Photo: Ron Tamminga.

Why Endurance?

Glen: "I like the challenge of completing the trail in all the various conditions. Also all the old and new friends I get to know at the rides."

Nancy: "I like the feeling I have when riding my horse. We become a team. I like meeting new people and seeing old friends. I try to ride for the challenge of the trail and to do my best that day with plenty left over for the next ride. I'm always looking forward to the next ride. Glen and I love the sport and our horses. We get to spend time together when we go to rides and we enjoy the people we meet."

Pam Loftus

Age: 38
Mileage: 1,000 miles
Profession: Registered nurse
Special Achievements:

- Completing four rides in the top ten in my second year of competition.

- Finishing with my horse "fit to continue"

"Mustangs are the greatest!" Photo: Pat Mitchell.

Why Endurance?

"The challenges of the trail, its natural elements, and the company of other riders are the reasons I enjoy endurance riding.

Your favorite horse?

"The joy I experience after a lot of hard work and learning is beyond words. The horse I ride, Mustang Hawk, was adopted from the BLM [Bureau of Land Management]. He was badly traumatized by his experiences in the prisoner training program and almost didn't make it. Today he is a wonderful, successful athlete who loves to go down the trail. He likes to be out front when he competes and I enjoy riding him there. I was afraid of him at first and had to learn to get 'quiet inside' in order to ride him. We've learned to trust each other and grow as a team through endurance riding."

Kathy Daley

Age: 42

Mileage: 1,500+

Profession: Certified Public Accountant

Special Achievements:

Ex-eventer turned avid endurance rider.

- Finishing the Tevis

- Top Ten on the Swanton Pacific 100 on my Thoroughbred

- Over fifteen finishes in the top ten on 50-mile rides.

- Being beaten by R. O. Grand Sultan (Rio) and finishing second in the Quicksilver 50

Why Endurance?

"The first time I tried an endurance ride I found out that a 'shotgun' start, wasn't a euphemism. They actually *fired* off a *gun* to start the ride. I didn't get control of my Thoroughbred again for 10 miles. By 40 miles he was 'out of gas' and I pulled him from the ride, and promptly went back to competing in three-day eventing. Now I absolutely love endurance riding and plan to stay active in it until I'm so old I can't mount a horse anymore!"

Your favorite horse?

"I ride a Thoroughbred mare named Bedazzle Her. At first I thought I'd make her into an event horse, but then I tried an endurance ride on her and she loved it! I use a lot of dressage in my training program to help control her during the rides. Thoroughbreds aren't for everyone. Bedazzle is pretty hot when she's in a race (and she thinks every ride is a race) and can be somewhat ornery. Her biggest problem is her feet, being a Thoroughbred. She has thin walls and soles and tends to get foot abscesses. She has a hard time keeping her shoes on. Riding her in endurance has been an exhilarating experience."

Hal Hall

Age: 42
Mileage: 6,000+
Profession: Banker
Special Achievements:

Three-time winner of the Tevis Cup Ride. Photo: Erik.

- Three-time winner of the Tevis Cup Ride
- Two-time winner of the Haggin Cup award for Best Condition at the Tevis
- Earned my 2,000-mile Tevis buckle by completing the ride twenty years
- My horse El Karbaj being named to the AERC Hall of Fame
- Over twenty-seven years of endurance riding with lots of top ten finishes

Why endurance?

"It's good wholesome outdoor recreation."

Your favorite horse?

"My horse El Karbaj and I have been doing this sport together for seventeen years. He's like one of the family. I never overworked or overtrained him and he finished his 13th Tevis at age twenty. I only retired him after he hurt himself in a fall in 1986. I don't ride him like I used to, but he's not ready for the old folks home yet! Endurance riding is a family affair for us; my wife Ann helps me with everything."

Genie Stewart-Spears

Age: 45

Mileage: 300

Profession: Equine journalist and photographer

Special Achievements:

Equine journalist and photographer. Photo: Genie Stewart-Spears.

- Finishing ninth overall and first lightweight on my half-Saddlebred/half-Fox Trotter, Commander's Lory, in our first event together: the 5-day, 285-mile New Mexico Renegade Ride

- Finishing in the top ten in the AERC Southeast Lightweight Division several years

Why Endurance?

"Because it's an individualist's sport and each ride is a personal accomplishment. The achievement is in traversing variable terrain in different weather and finding the personal best for yourself and your horse at every ride."

Your favorite horse?

"Lory is a no-nonsense type of horse who gets right down to business and covers the miles in the same steady, smooth trot that she struck up early in the morning. She is not a 'racer' but rather a 'touring' horse; but we still manage to do very well. My other horse, Heatzon, an Arab, I bred and raised myself. I owned his dam and bred to produce an endurance horse, and Heatzon loves a race to the finish line. At twelve, I have yet to uncover his full potential."

Julie Suhr and Bob Suhr

Age: Julie 72; Bob 78
Mileage: Julie 23,300; Bob 12,500
Profession: Both retired
Special Achievements:

- Julie: Best Condition at the Race Of Champions

- Julie: Three-time Haggin Cup winner (Best Condition on The Tevis Cup Ride)

- Julie: 20 Tevis completions

- Julie and Bob: Have competed on four continents

Three-time winner of the Haggin Cup (Tevis Best Condition Award). Photo: Pat Mitchell.

Why Endurance?

Julie: "Because since I was three years old, I have known the more time I spend on a horse the happier I am. The sport can make you feel ten feet tall one day and humble you the next. After 25 years of marriage, Bob decided he had better join the battle, so he climbed aboard a horse for the first time in his life at age 52, and completed his first ride, the Tevis Cup 100. Now he's as hooked on the sport as I am."

Seventy-eight-years-old and still going strong with 12,500 miles. Photo: Holly Ullyate.

Bob: "I've discovered the only way to spend long hours with the lovely lady who is my wife is to get out there and ride with her."

Your favorite horse?

Julie: "On the advice of a friend, I bought my Arabian, HCC Gazal, without ever having ridden him. He won the Haggin Cup for me three times! Gazal loves company, so he never wants to win because that means going off and leaving his buddies. His gait of choice is the lope. He is a totally kind and gentle horse who has always made me feel proud to be his friend and humble to be privileged to own such an incredible athlete. Bob and I have competed in endurance rides together in France, South Africa and Australia."

Bob: "My favorite horse was SS Myllany, an Arab gelding who didn't have to stay with the pack. I won the Castlerock ride on him in 1979. Shortly after that he was kicked while in pasture and broke his leg and we had to have him put down."

Nina Warren

Age: 50

Mileage: 8,000

Profession: Horse trainer

Special Achievements:

- AERC National Champion

- AERC Best Condition National Champion

- Hall of Fame Horse

- Winner ROC and Best Condition 1994

- Silver Medal Team North American Championships

AERC National Champion 1983. Photo: Pat Mitchell.

Why endurance?

"I have always loved horses and have ridden since I was a child. When I first heard about endurance riding, I was intrigued by the thought of a horse being able to go 50 to a 100 miles in a single day. I liked competing, but showing hunters—which is what I was doing—was very expensive. Endurance riding seemed to be a relatively uncomplicated and inexpensive type of competition, plus it gave me an excuse to ride all day!"

Your favorite horse?

"Amir Nizraff, my first horse, is my favorite. He is a truly phenomenal athlete and won for me right from the start. He guided me through my first year of endurance and won everything it was possible to win along the way, including 15 Best Condition awards. If I could have one wish, it would be to make him six years old again and have the trail looming ahead between those wise-guy ears."

Bonnie Mielke

Age: 48

Mileage: 14,000

Profession: Special education teacher

Special Achievements:

AERC First Middleweight
1995. Photo: Pat Mitchell.

- My horse Mocha being honored as AERC's Horse of the Year

- AERC Regional Middleweight Champion

- Five first-place finishes and Best Condition awards in 1996

Why endurance?

"I enjoy the mental and physical challenges of endurance riding. I love to ride on trails especially fast and enjoy competing. I also enjoy the camaraderie and sharing ideas."

Your favorite horse?

"Pieraaz came to me a headstrong horse with lots of bad habits, who wanted a person to give himself to. Last season I set a goal of finishing first on Pieraaz's last five rides and getting Best Condition on all of them. As we won each ride and got best condition, people talked more and more of the 'Pieraaz myth.' On the fourth ride, we rode alone all day because no one wanted to go that fast."

Pat Oliva

Age: 59

Mileage: 11,000

Profession: ER Nurse—retired

Special Achievements:

AERC National Middleweight Champion 1991.
Photo: Pat Mitchell.

- AERC National Middleweight Championship 1991

- AERC Rider Mileage Championship

- Top Ten Tevis Cup

Why Endurance?

"The very best thing about endurance is the people and friendships you develop. We are a competitive group, but I have seen the competitiveness cease as soon as someone needs help. Part of the thrill is putting your six hundred-dollar horse up against whatever's out there and having a good chance of winning."

Your favorite horse?

"I never owned a horse until I was 35. I tried a little showing and some cutting, but I got hooked on endurance riding. My half-Arab, Rushcreek Reid, has done some awesome stuff for me, including finishing third in the South Carolina 100 in eight hours and 13 minutes without a crew to help us, and then collecting the Best Condition award to boot. I bought "Shoney" when he was an unbroke two-year-old. He's retired now but, he and I still share trail time because I use him as my search and rescue horse."

FUN RIDES AND
SPECIAL EVENTS

Specific dates, and contact persons for all rides listed here and sanctioned by the American Endurance Ride Conference can be obtained by calling the AERC office in Auburn, California, or by consulting the ride calendar published in *Endurance News*, the official publication of AERC.

JANUARY—FEBRUARY

Far Out Forest

Distance:	35/50/100
Rating:	Challenging to difficult
Held:	First weekend in February
Location:	Florida, in the Ocala Forest
Weather:	Varies, 40° F. to 70° F., can be hot and humid
Base camp:	Beautiful spot on Doe Lake, in the forest. Lots of trees, showers, bathrooms, building for meetings and awards banquet, good road into base camp (about 1 1/2 miles from highway).

Trail:	Picturesque pine forest, deep sand, a few swampy places, rolling hills, no rocks, wide jeep trails and forest roads.
Notes:	Banquet is Friday before the ride. Completion, TT, BC and Weight Division awards.

Twenty Mule Team

Distance:	55/100
Rating:	Moderate
Held:	February
Location:	Southern California
Weather:	Ranges from warm (70s) to cold and windy
Base camp:	Flat open ground, no trees, some pipe corrals available, water available, toilets, paved access road
Trail:	Historic desert loop trail, passes through beautiful canyon, good footing. Water provided by ride management.
Notes:	Fifty percent completion rate.

MARCH—MAY

Biltmore

Distance:	25/50/100
Rating:	Moderate to challenging
Held:	May
Location:	North Carolina
Weather:	Beautiful spring weather, sometimes rainy
Base camp:	Primitive horse camping in large pasture, water for horses, no trees to tie to, close to the French Broad River, access road is long and narrow. Picturesque, Biltmore Estate in background.
Trail:	Wide, great footing, few rocks. Trails are 100-year-old carriage trails. Rolling, wooded hills, very well marked.
Notes:	Ride fills early every year (Feb.–Mar.), elaborate awards, good food. Saturday night dinner and awards breakfast on Sunday.

JUNE

The Old Dominion

Distance:	50/100
Rating:	Challenging to difficult
Held:	June
Location:	Fort Valley, Virginia
Weather:	Often hot and humid
Base camp:	4-H center, nice, grassy, some stalls available, pool, tennis courts, bathrooms, water.
Trail:	Scenic ride, held during spring, crosses the Shenandoah River, rocky, mountainous, can have swampy places, a lot of single-track. Trail climbs up Sherman Gap at 80 miles (most riders do this portion in the dark).
Notes:	Pads recommended. Buckle completion awards for 100.

JULY

Bandit Springs

Distance:	30/50/100
Rating:	Moderate to difficult
Held:	Third week in July
Location:	Oregon
Weather:	Sunny, dry 80° F., can also be hot and/or humid
Base camp:	1000-acre meadow, no trees to tie to, 2 1/2 miles off main highway on hard gravel, all-weather road, water from creek and provided by management.
Trail:	Winding, well-maintained trail through old-growth Ponderosa Pine forest, beautiful wild flowers, wild horses, elk and deer, 20-mile loop and 30-mile loop, repeated for 100 milers. Trail very well marked, lots of glow sticks after dark, lots of natural water on the trail. Lots of climbing and descending.

Notes: Night riding in heavily wooded area. Very nice T-shirts for completion awards.

Big Horn 100

Distance: 100 miles
Rating: Challenging
Held: July
Location: Shell, Wyoming
Weather: Varies, can snow or be hot
Base camp: Nestled along Shell Creek, trees, lots of water, portable toilet facilities, just off Highway 14.
Trail: One continuous loop, can be rocky in spots, single-track, rough. Big Horn National Forest, 5000-foot altitude gain during ride, plenty of water on well-marked trail, breathtaking scenery with lots of wildflowers.
Notes: Awards breakfast Sunday morning, blanket awards to TT, finishing awards. Ride was started in 1972.

Fireworks 50

Distance: 30/50
Rating: Moderate
Held: July or early August
Location: Santa Cruz mountains of California
Weather: Moderate to hot, fog in the morning
Base camp: Large equestrian show and trail-ride grounds, plenty of parking, good water, woods or open fields, some pens available, showers, toilets.
Trail: Beautiful wooded trail, lots of single-track, crosses streams and rivers, rolling, some climbs (not steep), some sand, good footing. Lunch and vet check on bluffs overlooking Pacific Ocean. Can be windy and chilly, especially early in the morning.
Notes: Fun ride, good food, banquet Saturday following the ride, dinner on Friday also available, controlled start, nice awards.

Race Of Champions

See **October—November—December** for listing.

Tevis Cup 100 Mile One-Day Ride

Distance:	100 miles
Rating:	Difficult
Held:	During full of the riding moon in July or August
Location:	Sierra Nevada Mountains of California
Weather:	Expect heat (up to 120° F.) in bottom of canyons
Base camp:	Robie Park, outside Truckee, Nevada. Plenty of parking in forest setting, water available in stock tanks, vetting held in a grassy meadow. Access road is dirt and gravel—long, very dusty, and narrow.
Trail:	Historic trail used by gold and silver miners during the 1850s, rugged, rocky, gorgeous, some parts remote and inaccessible. Can be treacherous after dark. Single-track trails (some very narrow) and fire roads, some riding down a main street through town of Forest Hill. Trail climbs to an elevation of 8,750 feet at Emigrant Pass. Includes climb over sheer rock, Cougar Rock, during first leg of ride. Over 18,000-foot altitude gain during the ride. Trail includes a river crossing, finishes at the fair grounds in Auburn, California. Mentally as well as physically challenging. Trail well marked.
Notes:	Pads recommended. Horses and riders need to be very fit. Fifty percent or less completion rate most years. Copyrighted silver buckle for completion. Crew needed. Crews not allowed at all check points. Cutoff times enforced. Ride limited to 250 entries. Awards banquet held early Sunday afternoon. Riders wanting to be in contention for the Haggin or Tevis Cup must weigh at least 165 pounds. Addictive to many riders.

Vermont 100

Distance: 100 miles

Rating: Challenging

Held: Third weekend in July

Location: South Woodstock, Vermont

Weather: Cool to hot (90° F.); moderate to high humidity

Base camp: In a private farm meadow, vetting in indoor arena, no trees to tie to, water in camp, showers, dirt access road.

Trail: Lots of dirt roads through shaded forest, some single-track. Riders cross a covered bridge. Some steep climbs, hilly terrain, great views.

Notes: Great hospitality, an awards breakfast Sunday morning, 100-mile run held with ride. Buckles for completion, also TT, BC and breed awards.

AUGUST

Swanton Pacific 100

Distance: 100 miles

Rating: Difficult

Held: August

Location: Mountain range along Pacific Ocean south of San Francisco

Weather: Temperature can vary greatly, generally moderate to hot

Base camp: Located in a canyon, can be cool at night. Long, narrow access road into camp—one-way traffic at spots. Grassy field camping surrounded by redwoods, lots of water in creek.

Trail: Beautiful, mountainous, goes through redwood forest, stunning views of entire North Coast in places, good footing, mixture of single-track trail and fire roads. Well marked.

Notes: Snacks for horses and riders at water stops. Sterling silver buckles available, but they must be purchased in addition to entry fee. Completion award is a plaque made from local wood with room for date plates.

Tevis Cup 100 Mile One Day Ride

See **July** entry.

SEPTEMBER

Kettle Moraine

Distance:	50/100
Rating:	Moderate
Held:	September
Location:	Wisconsin
Weather:	Varies, could be warm to cold
Base camp:	Camp on grass, lots of trees, running water with electricity, sheltered pens available, plenty of parking, gravel access road.
Trail:	Held during peak fall-color season, combination of maple trees and rolling hills. Rocky in places, wide, no steep hills, some swampy footing, well marked, lots of places for pit crews to meet rider. No glow bars at night.
Notes:	Ride held in very pretty area of Wisconsin, lots of vets. Awards dinner with trophy awards.

Paulina Peak

Distance:	30/60/100
Rating:	Challenging to difficult
Held:	September
Weather:	Ranges from 35° F. to 80s, occasionally snows on top of mountain

Base camp:	Forest Service campgrounds, lots of parking room, forest, dirt campground footing, plenty of water, good access road. Manure and hay must be bagged.
Trail:	Mountain trail, 2,000-foot climb in first nine miles, views of crater, lots of single-track, footing good, dirt and some cinders, can be dusty, well marked, deer and elk in deep forest.
Notes:	Well-run ride, well-marked trail, nice finishing awards, helpful ride management.

Virginia City 100

Distance:	100 miles
Rating:	Challenging to difficult
Held:	September
Location:	Western Nevada
Weather:	Moderate 70° F., occasional rain
Base camp:	Limited space, camping in the parking lot of a historic old ice house. Bathrooms, good access road, water.
Trail:	Very rocky terrain. Trail goes over Mt. Davidson at 8,000-foot altitude, offers 360° panoramic views. Home to wild horses, which have been known to travel with the riders for short distances.
Notes:	Pads recommended. Silver buckle for completion.

OCTOBER—NOVEMBER—DECEMBER

Carolina 30/50/100

Distance:	30/50 and 100 miles
Rating:	Easy to moderate
Held:	Saturday after Thanksgiving
Location:	Near Camden, South Carolina
Weather:	Cool, upper 30s to low 60s, frequently rains

Base camp: Woods and open fields, outdoor building with showers, plenty of water, highway access.

Trail: Mostly pine forest, sandy footing, flat to rolling terrain, water in ponds or ride-supplied.

Notes: Great hospitality, ride is fifteen years old and is attended by riders from a great many states, and also Canada. Completion awards vary from year to year. Meals are homemade and include Friday and Saturday dinner. Food available all day.

Race Of Champions

Distance: 100 miles

Rating: Challenging to difficult

Held: Usually in the summer or fall

Location: Moves around the country

Weather: Varies

Base camp: Varies with location

Trail: Always challenging, varies with location

Notes: Horses and riders have to qualify to enter. Known for its lavish awards, extracurricular activities and entertainment.

PASSPORTING YOUR HORSE FOR INTERNATIONAL COMPETITIONS

Riding at the international level involves more effort (and red tape) than taking your horse out for a 50-mile spin around the block. You will need to become a member of AERC and AERC International, and keep track of upcoming international events and their nomination dates. If your goal is to ride at this level someday, you can introduce yourself and your horse to the selectors by nominating yourself a year or two before you feel you might actually be picked as a rider to represent your zone or country in an event. Your horse must be eight years old before he can compete in an international event, such as the North American Championships or the World Championships. By nominating early, you will give the selectors a chance to watch your progress as you and your horse work toward your international goals

To nominate, you must fill out a form that gives your statistics. You will want to include a carefully kept record of the rides in which you and/or your horse have competed. You and your horse need at least a two-year paper trail showing evidence of six to ten successful 100-mile rides before you can expect to be taken seriously when you nominate. Select your rides to showcase your horse's strengths. If he is a great mountain horse, and the upcoming event in which you would like to compete is located in mountainous terrain, his record will work for him if you plan it that way in advance. You and your horse must finish strongly and consistently sound in order to be considered, but it is not necessary to win every time. It is a good idea to try to be in the top ten at least most of the time, as this will help you get noticed and remembered. A good strong horse, however, that occasionally places in the top twenty and rebounds in the next race to the top ten would certainly be considered by the selectors. How you handle your horse during the ride, trail strategy, vet check procedures, and so forth, as well as your own mental and physical state, will also influence selectors. Someone who is a tough competitor if everything is going well, but falls apart when something goes wrong is not going to be the first choice, despite a solid horse.

In order to compete in international events—whether on the continent or abroad—your horse will need a passport. Obtaining a horse passport can be a lengthy process, taking up to three months if all does not go well. Begin early and leave time for mistakes, especially if this is your first time. The owner must be a member of the American Horse Shows Association, and the horse must be recorded with the AHSA in order to get a passport. You can join, record the horse, and request your passport application all at once, by calling or writing the AHSA (AHSA, 220 East 42 Street, New York, NY 10017-5806/(212) 972-2472) and paying the appropriate membership fees. When you receive the application, you must fill it out and send it back to the AHSA office with the application fee ($275.00). They will then send you the passport form, which you will need to complete and return. A requirement is that a veterinarian must fill it out. It is advisable to select a vet who is familiar with the passporting process and has done a number of them. Even vets who regularly fill out passport forms sometimes make a mistake. *Be sure to read the instruction booklet.* It gives specific instructions that are very exacting on how to record such items as markings, scars, whorls, white skin and white hooves. The document is used for identification of your horse by ride officials and helps them insure no one substitutes one horse for another. If any of the information is incomplete, inaccurate or simply not done exactly as requested (all white must be recorded with red ink, all scars/marks need to be shown in black ink, and so forth), the passport will come back to you until it is correct (some riders have experienced having their forms sent back to them as many as three or four times before being accepted). If someone misses a slip-up on your horse's passport in the AHSA office, you could get to the event but be unable to compete!

Your horse's vaccination schedule must be entered into his/her passport. The rules of passporting a horse require two flu injections be given—spaced one to three months apart. It is important to follow this time frame exactly, or your passport will be rejected. If you think you are going to want to passport your horse, be sure to get the following information when your vet gives your horse its flu shots:

1. The manufacturer of the vaccine

2. The lot number of the vaccine

3. The expiration date of the vaccine

If any of these items are missing, you will have to have your horse revaccinated and that means at least a month's delay.

When your vet has filled in the passport, send it back to the AHSA for validation. If it is okay, they will validate it and return it to you.

When you arrive on the grounds of the event, you must have your passport ready to give to the official identifying veterinarian, or your Chef d' Equip. If event rules also require a negative Coggins or any other tests or vaccinations, the results of those tests must also be recorded in your passport and signed by your vet, and you will need a health certificate.

It costs about $500.00 (including the $275 AHSA fee mentioned earlier) to passport your horse. Passports are good for four years. If this amount is intimidating, you are probably not ready for competition at the international level. The time, effort, travel and cost are far greater at this type of event than at the local level of the sport.

RECOMMENDED RESOURCES LIST

BOOKS

America's Long Distance Challenge
Karen Paulo

A look at endurance riding through the eyes of an experienced competitor.

Publisher: Trafalgar Square Publishing
Price: $19.95

Beating Muscle Injuries for Horses
Jack Meagher

The author is an equine sports massage therapist who has worked on the elite equine athletes of the USET. The book is clear and logical in its presentation, enabling readers to both better understand and apply the principles of massage to their own horses and discipline.

Publisher: Hamilton Horse Associates (can be purchased from AERC)
Price: $12.95

The Bowed Tendon Book

Tom Ivers

Soup-to-nuts resource about how to care for tendons if they are stressed or injured.

Publisher: Russell Meerdink Company, Ltd.
Price: $24.95

Cavalletti

Reiner Klimke

Information, diagrams and distances about the use of cavalletti in improving the equine athlete.

Publisher: J.A. Allen & Co.
Price: $14.95

Centered Riding

Sally Swift

Many of the images used in this unique approach to riding are extremely useful to endurance riders, both for their own comfort and that of their horse. The book focuses on rider freedom and balance, which has a profound effect on the horse as well.

Publisher: Trafalgar Square Publishing
Price: $18.95

Conditioning Sport Horses

Hilary M. Clayton

Excellent intermediate to advanced reading on the physical preparation of the horse for various equestrian sports including endurance riding. For those who want a specific (days, hours, miles, etc.) conditioning regimen—here it is.

Publisher: Sport Horse Publications, Box 355 RPO, University Saskatoon, Saskatchewan, Canada 57N 4J8

Price: $44.95

Endurance Riding: From Beginning to Winning

Lew Hollander

More information about the sport of endurance riding from a winning rider/runner with over 10,000 miles. Interesting and candid comments about riding strategy.

Publisher: Green Mansions Inc.

Price: $13.95

Equine Drugs and Vaccines: A Guide for Owners and Trainers

Eleanor M. Kellon, V.M.D. and Thomas Tobin M.V.B., M.R.C.V.S.

A reference book worth its weight in gold. Each drug/substance the book lists is broken down into headings that give the generic name, a description of its purpose, various brand names, indications for use, dosages and route of administration, special precautions, side effects, drug interactions, pregnancy precautions and drug-testing implications.

Publisher: Breakthrough Publications

Price: $45.00

First Aid for Horses

Eleanor Kellon

A handy glove-compartment-size book with lots of color pictures and information about treating the various types of injuries to which horses are subject. Gives a summary of symptoms, treatment, rates severity of problems, and indicates when veterinary intervention is necessary.

Publisher: Breakthrough Publications

Price: $24.50

Fit to Finish: The Distance Rider's Guide to Personal Fitness and Nutrition

Jennifer Oltmann, et al.

Contains a "twelve-minute test of fitness," gives a home-strengthening program, and provides information on back care and nutrition.

Publisher: Alpine Publications
Price: $9.95

Healing Your Horse

Meredith L. Snader, V.M.D., et al.

All the information you'll ever want or need on alternative therapies such as acupuncture, chiropractic, homeopathy and massage, and their place in the care, training and competing of your horse.

Publisher: Howell Book House
Price: $25.00

Horse Gaits, Balance and Movement

Susan E. Harris

Contains vital, easily read and understood information on the biomechanics of balance in the horse. Prepares the reader for maximizing the horse's athletic talent and minimizing its chance of fatigue and injury. Also includes a chapter on rider balance.

Publisher: Howell Book House
Price: $27.50

Horse Owner's Field Guide to Toxic Plants

Sandra Burger

A great guide to plants that are poisonous to horses, this book comes in a handy glove-compartment size. Includes color photographs of each poisonous plant, shows their geographic distribution, gives signs of poisoning and recommendations for what to do.

Publisher: Breakthrough Publications
Price: $22.50

101 Arena Exercises

Cherry Hill

While work on the trail is a necessary part of every distance horse's education, work in the "classroom" (arena) is equally important to develop the horse's ability to remain supple, sound, mentally settled and perform at the peak of his inherent biomechanical ability. Here is a book that assists the rider in knowing what to do with the time spent in the ring. Each page diagrams a gymnastic exercise, tells how to ride it, what to look for in the horse's performance, and cautions how the exercise might go wrong. Another must-have for the success-focused rider/competitor.

Publisher: Storey Publishing
Price: $29.95

Physical Therapy and Massage for the Horse

Jean-Marie Denoix and Jean-Pierre Pailloux

An outstanding book to help you understand the roles that muscle groups play in the ability of the horse to do his job well and stay sound. Great diagrams, with chapters on treatment organized by area of the body and preparation of muscles for specific types of competition.

Publisher: Trafalgar Square Publishing
Price: $29.95

Stretching

Bob Anderson

Contains well-illustrated line drawings on the subject of fitness through stretching exercises.

Publisher: Shelter Publications, Inc.
Price: $13.00

Tendon and Ligament Injuries in the Horse

David W. Ramey, D.V.M.

More information about those all-important legs, with very good structural diagrams and information on diagnosis through ultrasound scan.

Publisher: Howell Book House
Price: $14.95

Winning Strategies for Endurance Horse Racing

Courtney Hart

An in-depth analysis of the various elements impacting the sport of endurance racing.

Publisher: Writo, P.O. Box 1403, Los Gatos, CA, 95031
Price: $25.00

Veterinary Manual for the Performance Horse

Nancy Loving, D.V.M.

A must-have book for anyone in the sport. Includes information on conditioning the performance horse, hoof care, long-distance trailering, nutrition, confinement stress and other important topics. Written by an endurance vet with direct knowledge of the demands placed on the equine athletes in our sport.

Publisher: Equine Research Inc.
Price: $75.00

WEB SITES

American Endurance Ride Conference

http://www.aerc.org
Governing body for the sport of endurance in the United States of America.

Centered Riding

http://www.centeredriding.org

Information, instructor's list, and clinic dates & locations.

Donna Snyder-Smith

http://www.endurance.net/RightRider

Education, vacation and consulting services.

Endurance Net

http://www.endurance.net

Information concerning the sport of endurance riding.

TTEAM®

http://www.tteam-ttouch.com
http://www.LindaTellington-Jones.com

Information about TTEAM including clinic dates, locations and products.

Ride Camp

http://www.endurance.net/RideCamp

A distance riders chat group.

INDEX